EUROPEAN CARTOGRAPHERS AND THE OTTOMAN WORLD

1500–1750

Jan Vermeer van Delft (1632–1675). *The Geographer*. Courtesy of The Städel Museum, Frankfurt/Artothek

EUROPEAN CARTOGRAPHERS AND THE OTTOMAN WORLD

1500–1750

MAPS FROM THE COLLECTION OF O. J. SOPRANOS

IAN MANNERS

with a contribution by

M. PINAR EMİRALİOĞLU

THE ORIENTAL INSTITUTE MUSEUM OF THE UNIVERSITY OF CHICAGO

Library of Congress Control Number: 2007935787
ISBN: 978-1-885923-53-0
ISBN: 1-885923-53-8

The Oriental Institute, Chicago

Oriental Institute Museum Publications No. 27

This volume has been published in conjunction with the exhibition
European Cartographers and the Ottoman World, 1500–1750:
Maps from the Collection of O. J. Sopranos.

Published by The Oriental Institute of the University of Chicago
1155 East 58th Street
Chicago, Illinois 60637 USA
oi.uchicago.edu

Front Cover Illustration:

Georg Braun and Frans Hogenberg. *Byzantivm nunc Constantinopolis.* [1572].
From *Civitates Orbis Terrarum*, Cologne. The O. J. Sopranos Collection

Back Cover Illustration:

Abraham Ortelius. *Tvrcici Imperii Descriptio.* [1579].
From *Theatrum Orbis Terrarum.* [Antwerp], 1602.
The O. J. Sopranos Collection

Cover Design:

Hanau-Strain, Inc., Chicago

This volume was made possible through the generous donation of the Dellenback Family Foundation.

Printed by M&G Graphics, Chicago, Illinois.

The paper used in this publication meets the minimum requirements of American National Standard for
Information Service — Permanence of Paper for Printed Library Materials, ANSI Z39.48-1984
∞

TABLE OF CONTENTS

LIST OF FIGURES

FOREWORD

GIL J. STEIN
DIRECTOR, ORIENTAL INSTITUTE

The Oriental Institute's mission as a research center is one of discovery — the exploration of ancient Near Eastern civilizations through archaeological and textual studies, and the communication of this research to both scholars and the general public. The Institute's museum plays a key role in this process through its permanent galleries, and through our program of presenting two special exhibits each year. Our special exhibit European Cartographers and the Ottoman World, 1500-1750: Maps from the Collection of O. J. Sopranos provides visitors with a unique perspective on a crucial chapter in the history of this discovery — the revolutions in cartographic science that permitted European scientists and explorers to visualize the Near East in spatially accurate ways, while fitting it into their own cognitive maps of where and who they were. We simply cannot understand past times without what we might call the rationalization of space.

In a very real sense, the advances in mapmaking exemplified in this exhibit re-cast the Ottoman empire in a way that made possible the modern explorations of the archaeologists, philologists, and historians who have rediscovered the civilizations of the ancient Near East.

The maps in this exhibit are some of the masterpieces in the collection of O. J. (Jim) Sopranos, a long-time friend of the Oriental Institute and the current Chair of our Visiting Committee. Jim's interest in maps and in archaeology are two complementary facets of his lifelong fascination with geography, exploration, and history of the Mediterranean world. Jim Sopranos dedicates the exhibit of his maps to his cousin and fellow travel adventurer, the late George B. Javaras. My colleagues and I deeply appreciate his vision in sharing these highlights from his collection with the public, and in his generous support of the exhibit itself. In doing so, he has provided us all with a perspective that we would normally not be able to see. I would also like to thank Museum Director Geoff Emberling, Coordinator of Special Exhibits Emily Teeter, and Guest Curator Ian Manners for the outstanding job in planning this exhibit and in shepherding it through to become a physical reality.

PREFACE

GEOFF EMBERLING
DIRECTOR, ORIENTAL INSTITUTE MUSEUM

The permanent galleries of the Oriental Institute Museum display the prehistory and history of the ancient Middle East in each of its major regions. With the opening the Marshall and Doris Holleb Family Gallery for Special Exhibits in February, 2006, the museum inaugurated a program of special exhibits. We now have the flexibility to present specific topics in greater detail, to develop comparative themes that cross regions, to display recent discoveries and research insights, and to expand beyond the temporal and geographical limits in ways that enhance interest in and understanding of the ancient world. All these possibilities allow the museum to reach wider audiences with exhibits of broad appeal and great interest.

Maps are small worlds that both represent geographical space and at the same time postulate a relationship of human mapmakers and map-users to that world. European Cartographers and the Ottoman World, 1500–1750, at one level shows the development of cartography from fifteenth- to sixteenth-century maps based on observations gathered by Ptolemy in the second century A.D. to the scientific maps of the eighteenth century.

In another sense, it is an exhibit that explores ways of knowing and representing other lands and other cultures, a theme that resonates throughout the study of the ancient world. The opportunity to trace a systematic development in one such cultural relationship is rare in collections from ancient times and is particularly welcome here. The relationship between "east" and "west" has had an urgent relevance in recent years, and it is refreshing to learn that cartographers, at least, shared knowledge across this divide during a time of intense cultural, economic, and political interaction.

Emily Teeter, the Oriental Institute Special Exhibits Coordinator, first developed the idea for this exhibit in 2003 while visiting the home of O. J. (Jim) and Angie Sopranos, where she admired his collection of these beautiful, fascinating, and illuminating maps. As plans developed, she contacted Ian Manners, Professor of Geography and Middle Eastern Studies at the University of Texas, Austin, to ask if he would consider curating the exhibit. Soon after his first visit to Chicago, in 2005, he proposed expanding the exhibit with a piece from the Oriental Institute and loans from the Special Collections Research Center of the University of Chicago Library, the Newberry Library in Chicago, and the Walters Art Museum in Baltimore. Over three more extremely productive (and enjoyable) visits to Chicago, Ian shaped the exhibit and catalogue to their present form. It was a happy coincidence that our timetable coincided with the Chicago Festival of Maps, a city-wide celebration of cartography.

It is truly a pleasure to thank everyone who has made this exhibit and catalogue a standard to aspire to in the future.

To Ian Manners, for outstanding curatorial work — intellectual brilliance, respect for deadlines, and friendliness rarely go together with such grace.

To Jim Sopranos, for the maps, for organizational support, and for being such a generous host.

To Emily Teeter, for developing the idea of the exhibit and for making it all happen with unfailing curatorial eye, energy, and good cheer.

To Dianne Hanau-Strain of Hanau-Strain Associates, for sympathetic and visually striking design work.

To M. Pınar Emiralioğlu, for her contribution to the catalogue and to Cornell Fleischer, for his wise advice.

To the dedicated staff of the Oriental Institute Museum, for skill and grace under pressure: Erik Lindahl (Head Preparator), Alison Whyte (Lead Conservator); Helen McDonald (Registrar); Tom James (Curatorial Assistant); Jean Grant and Marcy Montross (Photographers); and Carole Krucoff (Head of Education).

To Leslie Schramer and Thomas Urban in the Oriental Institute's Publications Office, who have done their usual outstanding work with, for once, enough time to do it in.

To our colleagues at lending institutions:

The University of Chicago Library Special Collections Research Center:

Alice Schreyer (Director), Patti Gibbons (Preservation Manager), and Kerri Sancomb (Exhibition Specialist)

The Newberry Library:

Robert W. Karrow, Jr. (Curator of Special Collections and Curator of Maps), Lauren Reno (Program Assistant), and Giselle Simon (Director of Conservation Services)

The Walters Art Museum:

William Noel (Curator of Manuscripts and Rare Books)

Finally, and certainly not least, to Robert and Geraldine Dellenback of the Dellenback Family Foundation, for sponsorship of the catalogue and the Replogle Foundation, for support of the exhibit and map symposium to be held December 8, 2007, at the Oriental Institute.

AUTHOR'S ACKNOWLEDGMENTS

Numerous colleagues and friends have helped me in preparing this catalogue. My debt to them and the many students who have challenged me to develop and refine my ideas over many years is enormous. I would like to express my particular gratitude to Samer Ali, Dinis Cosgrove, Kay Ebel, Pınar Emiralioğlu, and Robert Karrow for sharing so generously their expertise and knowledge, filling the empty spaces in my own mental map while saving me from errors. I owe special thanks to Margaret Lynch for her careful and insightful reading of an earlier draft of the manuscript. I benefited enormously from the resources and skill of the staffs at The Newberry Library, Chicago; the Special Collections Research Center at the Regenstein Library of the University of Chicago; and the Harry Ransom Humanities Research Institute at the University of Texas at Austin. The challenge of curating the exhibit and preparing the catalogue was made immensely more enjoyable by the help and support I received from Geoff Emberling, Emily Teeter, and the staff of the Oriental Institute Museum. I am greatly indebted to Thomas Urban, Leslie Schramer, and Dianne Hanau-Strain for the patience and creativity they brought to the editing and design of the catalogue. Finally, and most importantly, this project could not have been completed without the encouragement of Jim Sopranos. He has responded with infinite patience to my many questions, has been an indefatigable researcher in tracking down details about several of the maps, and has inspired the project with his enthusiasm and passion for maps.

INTRODUCTION TO THE EXHIBIT

IAN MANNERS
PROFESSOR OF GEOGRAPHY AND MIDDLE EASTERN STUDIES
THE UNIVERSITY OF TEXAS AT AUSTIN

The exhibit European Cartographers and the Ottoman World, 1500–1750: Maps from the Collection of O. J. Sopranos explores how mapmakers came to know and map the Ottoman world between the fifteenth and eighteenth centuries. It opens with the intellectual and geographical discoveries of the fifteenth century that undermined the medieval view of the cosmos and illustrates how mapmakers sought to produce and map a new geography of the world, one that reconciled classical ideas and theories with contemporary information brought back by travelers and voyagers.

The authority of Ptolemy's *Geographia*, translated into Latin for the first time in the early fifteenth century, was at times stifling, but the world and regional maps constructed using Ptolemy's mathematical principles and geometric grid provided a radically different picture of the habitable world from earlier religious *mappae mundi*. Yet Ptolemy's geographical knowledge dated from the late Roman period, a world that was being transformed for European mapmakers by the discovery of new continents. The intellectual and scholarly excitement with Ptolemy's spatial order developed alongside a very different mapping tradition, one that had its roots in practical seafaring and the navigational needs of sailors. The resulting tension between the old learning and the new, between geographical knowledge derived from classical cosmographical theories and texts and the practical knowledge of voyagers and travelers, is perhaps the defining characteristic of fifteenth- and sixteenth-century cartography (Campbell, *Earliest Printed Maps*, p. 1).

As part of this story, the exhibit points to the remarkably close relationship that existed between the new centers of intellectual and artistic inquiry in Renaissance Europe and the Ottoman world during the fifteenth and sixteenth centuries. Indeed, the Ottoman empire was seen by contemporaries as very much part of Europe in this early modern period, not only as the successor to the Roman-Byzantine empires, but also as a polity directly involved in the struggle for power and influence in Europe. For much of the sixteenth century, the central element in European politics was the confrontation between the Ottomans and the Habsburg dynasty. This occurred both along the Hungarian borders of the Austrian branch of the Habsburgs, and in the central Mediterranean with the Spanish branch of the same dynasty. That this created political alliances that cut across cultural differences is apparent in the French-Ottoman *entente*. This was pursued with varying degrees of enthusiasm during the sixteenth century and continued to be revived at times up until the late seventeenth century (Faroqhi, *Ottoman Empire and the World*, p. 33). The image of an Ottoman fleet commanded by the corsair-turned-admiral Hayreddin Barbarossa overwintering in the French port of Toulon and cooperating in an attack on the town of Nice (allied with the Habsburgs) in 1543 illustrates the complexity of European-Ottoman political relations. But beyond the political and military confrontation there was convergence, notably through trade within the Mediterranean basin and through artistic and intellectual exchanges (Goffman, *Ottoman Empire and Early Modern Europe*).

Mapmaking was affected by these exchanges, but it also contributed to them. Copies of Ptolemy's works were valued by Ottoman rulers and Italian princes alike. Ottoman sailors and navigators such as Piri Re'is made significant contributions to the charting of the Mediterranean. Ottoman geographies such as the *Tarih-i Hindi-i Garbi* were every bit as global in their vision, scope, and information as those being produced by their western neighbors. Clearly, the circulation of maps, texts, and geographical information did not stop at the borders of the sultan's territories, and interest in the new language of cartography was as great in Istanbul as it was in Venice and Lisbon. A central thrust of the exhibit therefore has been to explore the ways in which mapping and the production of new geographical knowledge in the fifteenth and sixteenth centuries were shaped by intricate and sometimes surprising cultural interactions between the Ottoman world and the rest of Europe.

The exhibit further traces the evolution of mapmaking and the contexts in which maps were used through the work of such cartographers as Giacomo Gastaldi and Abraham Ortelius, whose sixteenth-century maps and atlases were conceived and seen as mirrors held up to nature, and of Nicolas Sanson and Guillaume de L'Isle in the seventeenth and eighteenth centuries, whose maps both reflected and shaped changing European conceptions of political territory and national identity.

These later maps increasingly embody the political, commercial, and scientific interests of European nation-states. The emerging scientific mode of Enlightenment mapping, particularly the weight placed on instrumentation and measurement as a means of achieving more accurate spatial representation, is particularly evident in the work of French cartographers. Their work greatly enlarged the scope of cartography in the service of the state and had far-reaching implications for the ways in which Europeans came to imagine and visualize Ottoman territories in Europe and Asia. It is with the impact of Enlightenment ideas on the demarcation and mapping of Ottoman borders and territories, and the role of maps as "vehicles for conceptual and visual possession" (Livingstone, *Geographical Tradition*, p. 52), that the exhibit concludes.

To illustrate these developments, twenty-six sheet maps and a variety of atlases and travel narratives have been selected. These include illuminated manuscript sea charts and atlases, the earliest printed maps of the Ottoman empire, an Ottoman sea atlas, bird's-eye views of cities that were intended to provide those who wished to avoid the rigors and dangers of travel with the experience of knowing distant places as if from life, a rare Ottoman printed atlas from the nineteenth century, decorative regional maps, a Mediterranean chart that has been described as the finest example of Dutch map art, and sketches, memoirs, and reports from travelers whose observations and descriptions of the Ottoman world enabled cartographers to update their maps. Collectively, they demonstrate the power of maps to shape geographical knowledge of that part of the world we know today as the Middle East.

Map of Europe and the Ottoman World, ca. 1600

EUROPEAN CARTOGRAPHERS AND THE OTTOMAN WORLD

IAN MANNERS

Among the many efforts by cartographers to visualize and represent the world as it was becoming known to Europe in the sixteenth century, the heart-shaped world map of Oronce Fine (1494–1555) is undoubtedly the most visually arresting.[1] Here, "in the first heart of Oronce," is an elegant answer to the challenge of representing on paper a world radically altered as a result of the geographical and intellectual discoveries of the Renaissance. Fine's cosmographic heart also conveyed a certain moral authority, and for many scholars its unifying vision of the world transformed into a human heart symbolized the new spirit of humanist inquiry and its potential for transcending the profound religious and political divisions existing within Europe (Cosgrove, *Apollo's Eye*, p. 133; Mangani, "Abraham Ortelius"). Of the maps based on Fine's 1534 woodcut, one of the most intriguing is the work sometimes referred to as the "lost" Turkish map of Hajji Ahmed, not least for what it reveals about the cultural and intellectual landscape of early modern Europe (fig. 1).

The title, in large woodcut Arabic script, describes the map as "A Complete and Perfect Map Describing the Whole World" (Karrow, *Mapmakers*, pp. 172–73). The accompanying text, in Ottoman Turkish, indicates this is the work of a certain Hajji Ahmed of Tunis, who "on seeing this really excellent and important work, and realizing that it was of value and essential to all the Moslems and their rulers ... translated it systematically from the language and script of the Franks into [their] script" (the translated passages are from Ménage, "Map of Hajji Ahmed"). In advancing the claims of his map, Hajji Ahmed says that he has been inspired by the words of the early fourteenth-century Arab cosmographer Abu al-Fida regarding the importance of geographical knowledge to rulers and princes; in this spirit he has prepared a map that will provide such necessary knowledge for those newly discovered lands unknown to Abu al-Fida. Hajji Ahmed informs us that he studied law in the *medreses* of the city of Fez in the Maghreb, and had "devoted [his] life to the zealous and persistent pursuit of learning and wisdom and an honorable name" (Ménage, "Map of Hajji Ahmed," p. 297). Unhappily, it had been his misfortune to be taken captive by the "Franks" and brought to Italy, where he sought to use his scholarship and learning in preparing the Turkish translation of the map, "for this language is the most dominant in the world," in the hope that, despite its imperfections, this work this would earn him his freedom.

But Hajji Ahmed's map is not quite what it appears to be at first reading. Ménage's careful analysis of the text has revealed that the "Turkish in which the map is written is barbarous in the extreme," while the misspellings and grammatical mistakes are so pervasive "that it is frequently difficult to establish the sequence of thought" (Ménage, "Map of Hajji Ahmed," p. 299). Nor does the author's knowledge of Arabic, his claimed native language, appear to be much better. "We can safely conclude that the author was not the educated Tunisian that he purports to be" (ibid., p. 301). Who, then, was Hajji Ahmed? Did he even exist? If he was not the author, who was? And for whom was the "Turkish" map intended?

In fact the map was almost certainly prepared in Venice around 1559 (the text includes the date 967 after the Hegira [A.H.], which corresponds to A.D. 1559/1560). Most of the geographical information included on the map has been taken from European sources, notably Giovanni Battista Ramusio's great travel compendium *Delle Navigationi et Viaggi*, which had been published in Venice during the 1550s.[2] The evidence of European influence in both the content and language of the map suggested to Ménage that the map was actually a commercial venture involving three Venetians: Nicolò Cambi, Michele Membré (a friend of Ramusio's who for a long period in the second half of the sixteenth century was the official Turkish translator for the Venetian Republic), and a local printer, Marc Antonio Giustinian. In 1568 Giustinian was licensed by the Venetian authorities to print and sell a world map in Arabic (that is, the Arabic script), containing the observations of "Sultan Ismael" [Abu al-Fida] as compiled by "cagi Acmet" and translated by "Membré et Cambi and brought to perfection at last after a long delay" (Ménage, "Map of Hajji Ahmed," p. 308). But the language of the map, the care taken by the authors to use the correct honorifics for the Ottoman sultan, and the praise heaped upon him (and to a lesser extent on the Safavid shah), make it very clear that the intention was to secure Ottoman, and perhaps even Safavid, clients and patrons.[3]

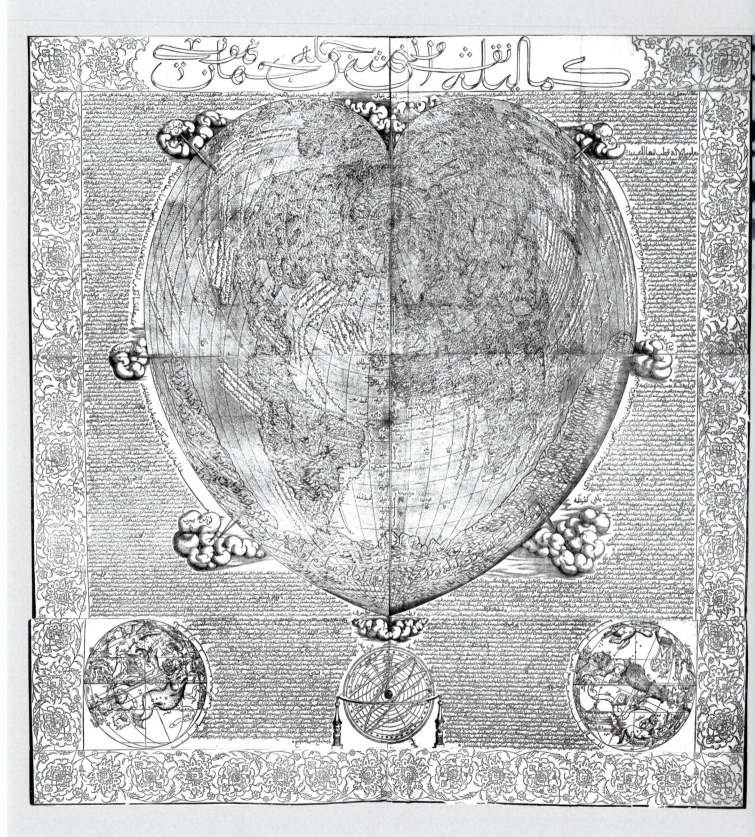

FIGURE 1. [Hajji Ahmed]. [*A Complete and Perfect Map Describing the Whole World*]. Cordiform ("heart-shaped") map with text in Ottoman Turkish. Printed in 1795 from blocks prepared in Venice ca. 1559. Novacco 8F 011. The Newberry Library, Chicago (Franco Novacco Map Collection)

Unfortunately for Giustinian, the venture proved ill fated. Relations between the Venetian city-state and the Ottomans deteriorated sharply late in 1568, and perhaps on this account he was called before the authorities, although Arbel ("Maps of the World," p. 25) suggests that other motivations were involved in the investigation which followed an accusation over the printing of Hebrew books. The unhappy outcome, however, was that Giustinian's license to print the map was revoked and the woodblocks and all copies of the map confiscated.[4] Nevertheless, the story behind the map illustrates how the new geographies of the late fifteenth and early sixteenth centuries were shaped by complicated (and sometimes surprising) intellectual, commercial, and political exchanges between the Ottoman world and the rest of Europe.[5]

Mapping in this early modern world should be seen as an activity that spanned the Mediterranean, and interest in the new language and content of maps was as great in Istanbul as it was in Venice and Lisbon. Arbel, for example, has uncovered documents in the Venetian archives showing that in the early 1550s three sons of Sultan Süleyman I — Bayezid, Mustafa, and Selim — had each independently approached the Venetian authorities about acquiring a world map (Arbel, "Maps of the World"). One of these documents, dated 1553, expresses the Venetian Senate's desire to "gratify the Lord Sultan Selim [later Sultan Selim II], son of the most Serene Lord Turk," and instructs the city's leading cartographer, Giacomo Gastaldi, to undertake the commission and prepare the world map "requested by [Selim] so insistently" (quoted in ibid., p. 22). Arbel sees a connection between these requests and the increasingly contentious struggle among Süleyman's sons in the early 1550s over the succession, a struggle in which the acquisition of a *mappa mundi* might have been seen as a symbolic means of expressing imperial authority.[6] But the broader context is the way in which maps were one element in an extraordinarily intricate web of relationships between western Europe and the Ottoman world. The Ottomans were not isolated from the intellectual currents and preoccupations of the period, and were active contributors to geographical thought and inquiry, and to the new world view that emerged (Brotton, *Trading Territories*).

MAPPING AND DISCOVERY DURING THE RENAISSANCE

In the fifteenth century, European knowledge of the world was reshaped by a series of momentous events that first undermined and then destroyed the medieval view of the cosmos. Donald Lach (*Asia*, p. 84) eloquently describes the shattering impact of the voyages made under Portuguese and Spanish patronage which demonstrated to Europeans "that the oceans were not impassable and that 'New Worlds' of unforeseen dimensions and promise lay open to those with the courage to seek them out." But as Lach emphasizes, the fifteenth century was equally a period of shattering intellectual discovery as humanist scholars and thinkers became re-acquainted with knowledge of the classical world through translations into Latin of a corpus of Greek texts. "The revelations of the classical past and the East were related events, not only because they were spread simultaneously, but also because they both helped to unsettle traditional attitudes and to bring about the intellectual orientation which we call 'modern'" (ibid., p. 84).

Mapping was central to these events. There was the technical challenge of recording and representing the flood of geographical information, and the equally daunting task of reconciling the newly acquired knowledge of the classical past with the practical observations of seamen and travelers.

> Steeped in classical learning, even universal minds ... were not always aware of new information from non-classical sources, and when they were, they were frequently skeptical about it. The diffusion of the Ptolemaic texts, for example, helped to raise questions about the new geographical information which sometimes brought the old and the new knowledge into direct conflict. It should not be surprising therefore that knowledge of the East from classical sources continued to leave its imprint on men who, often rightly, distrusted the more recent and sometimes conflicting information contained in the accounts of missionaries and travelers (Lach, *Asia*, p. 85).

Swept up by the intellectual currents of the century, mapmakers were, in a most fundamental sense, responding to and helping shape new ways of visualizing and knowing the world. The Oriental Institute Special Exhibit

European Cartographers and the Ottoman World, 1500–1750: Maps from the Collection of O. J. Sopranos illustrates the contributions of mapmakers to these intellectual and practical undertakings. In particular, it explores the influence of maps and mapping on the relationship between "western" Europe and the Ottoman world beginning in the fifteenth century and continuing through the end of the eighteenth century.

THE "REDISCOVERY" OF PTOLEMY

At the risk of simplifying what was an extraordinarily complicated history, the new maps and atlases that began to appear at the end of the fifteenth century were inspired and informed by three sources. First, there was the influence of Ptolemy's *Geographia*, knowledge of which re-entered the mainstream of European intellectual thought in the early fifteenth century.[7] Second, there were the accounts and narratives of travelers and voyagers, for whom observation trumped classical authority. And third, there was the well-established tradition of charting, most fully developed in the Mediterranean, that incorporated sailors' first-hand knowledge and practical experience of the sea (Campbell, "Portolan Charts," p. 372).

Translated into Latin for the first time around 1406 by Jacopo d'Angelo, the *Geographia* struck with "the force of a revelation" (Campbell, *Earliest Printed Maps*, p. 4), profoundly altering ideas about the known world and ways in which that "new" world could be represented (Edgerton, *Linear Perspective*, pp. 97–99). It is difficult for us, living in a world saturated with visual images, to appreciate just how astonishing Ptolemy's maps must have appeared to those who saw them for the first time in the fifteenth century. We might come close to capturing that sense of revelation by recalling the impact of the first images of earth seen as a small planet hanging in a vast velvet emptiness that were transmitted back in the course of the *Apollo 8* space mission (Cosgrove, "Contested Global Visions"). In practical terms, what Ptolemy offered was both a system of geographical coordinates — in effect latitude and longitude — that could be used to organize geographical information and determine spatial relationships on the earth's surface, plus a remarkable gazetteer comprising the coordinates of nearly eight thousand places determined in great part through direct astronomical observations. "It was perhaps because of its vast list of place names and its severe dedication to the careful compilation of cartographic data that the *Geographia* became the prototype for all similar endeavors until the end of the sixteenth century" (Lach, *Asia*, p. 69). But the *Geographia* also had a moral imperative, for as Edgerton has observed ("Mental Matrix," p. 14), its organizing system seemed to offer scholars a way of uncovering the geometric order and harmony that must surely underlie the earth's apparent diversity.

In a parallel exhibit, the Newberry Library of Chicago has displayed a copy of most of the printed editions of the *Geographia*, but the smaller subset of Ptolemaic maps and atlases included in the present exhibit also serve to illustrate the way in which Ptolemy's work established a new visual language for cartography during the fifteenth century. Through the new medium of printing, Ptolemy's ideas and images became familiar to a wider audience. An indication of its early authority is to be found in the frequency with which the text and accompanying maps were reproduced, with a total of four printed editions (plus two reprints) appearing even before the end of the fifteenth century (Campbell, *Earliest Printed Maps*, pp. 122–38).[8] Nearly every mapmaker of distinction in the first half of the sixteenth century — including Giacomo Gastaldi, Sebastian Münster, and Martin Waldseemüller — was involved in preparing maps for editions of the *Geographia*, and it was really only the publication of Abraham Ortelius' *Theatrum Orbis Terrarum* in 1570 that effectively ended reliance on Ptolemy's maps as an authoritative picture of the world (Karrow, *Mapmakers*, p. 397).

The inset essay, *"Asia Propria" in Fifteenth- and Sixteenth-Century Ptolemaic Atlases*, discusses in more detail how these early cartographers depicted the lands around the eastern Mediterranean that were then under Ottoman rule. Although the visual and artistic differences between these maps is often quite striking, because all were inspired and informed by the same source it should not be surprising that they exhibit a similar underlying structure and organization (figs. 2–5, see essay *"Asia Propria"*, below). Moreover, in terms of the geographical content of the maps, for the most part what is shown is Ptolemy's geography of the late Roman period. The silence of these maps with respect to political and cultural developments in "Asia Propria" during the fifteenth century is particularly noticeable. The best cartographers of the period, such as Bernardus Sylvanus and Martin Waldseemüller, sought to update maps or include *tabulae novae* that removed many of the imagined topographies and outdated classical toponyms

"ASIA PROPRIA" IN FIFTEENTH- AND SIXTEENTH-CENTURY PTOLEMAIC ATLASES

The first printed maps of the region that Renaissance cartographers identified as "Asia Propria" or "Asia Minor" appear in the earliest editions of Ptolemy's *Geographia* that began to circulate in Europe in the late fifteenth century. A fine example of this map is the woodcut with hand-cut lettering from the 1486 Ulm edition printed by Johann Reger (fig. 2). With its delicate coloring and artistic elegance, the map, entitled *Prima Asie Tabvla*, typifies the distinctive style and geographic conventions found on the twenty-six regional maps that made up the traditional Ptolemaic canon. The different techniques and map projections employed, as well as the varying skills of the craftsmen who produced the maps, can result in quite striking visual and aesthetic differences in the maps appearing in the early printed editions of the *Geographia* (Campbell, *Earliest Printed Maps*, p. 125). Thus the Ulm edition used woodcut blocks, reflecting the German experience with this medium, and the maps are drawn using the trapezoid projection developed by Nicolaus Germanus in the mid-fifteenth century (in which the parallels and meridians are drawn as straight lines but with the meridians converging toward the poles). By way of contrast, the maps that accompany the 1482 *Geographia*, prepared by Francesco di Nicolò Berlinghieri, were printed from copper plates. Here, the poor quality of the workmanship, particularly the uneven lettering and cluttered appearance with extended and broken inscriptions that frequently double back on themselves, makes the map of

FIGURE 2. [Claudius Ptolemy]. *Prima Asie Tabvla.* 1486. From the Ulm printing of the *Geographia* by Johann Reger. The O. J. Sopranos Collection

Asia Minor much more difficult to comprehend (fig. 3). The maps from Bernardus Sylvanus' 1511 edition of the *Geographia*, printed in Venice, illustrate the technical advances in printing that were proceeding hand in hand with the new cartography (fig. 4). This was the first Ptolemy "atlas" to use two-color printing (black and red) and (very rare for an atlas from this period) has maps printed on both sides of the page (Karrow, *Mapmakers*, p. 522).

Despite these external differences, the maps were inspired by the same text and their geographies compiled from the same listing of place names. As a result, their content and the internal arrangement and organization of geographic information shows little variation. While the coastline of modern Turkey is generally recognizable, other features of the map, such as the island of Cyprus, are badly distorted. Dominating the map are the extended solid arcs (highlighted in a light brown on the Ulm map) symbolizing mountains that stretch chain-like across large sections of the map. A curious feature found on several maps is the doorway cut into the "Amanvs mons" in south-central Anatolia with the inscription "Porte Syrie." This is clearly the cartographer's representation of the Cilician Gates, the pass across the Taurus mountains that for centuries provided a natural route connecting interior Anatolia with Syria and the eastern Mediterranean. In this inscription, as in the regional divisions and other place names, is a clear reminder of the classical sources that were used in compiling the map.

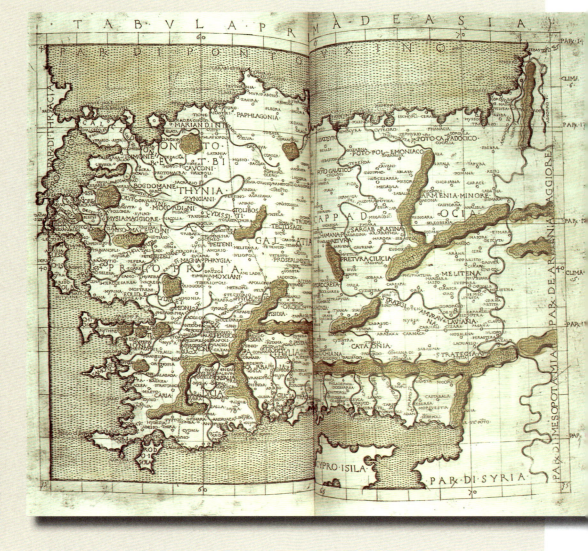

FIGURE 3. Francesco di Nicolò Berlinghieri. *Tabvla Prima de Asia.* [1482]. From Berlinghieri's *Geographia* printed in Florence by Nicolas Laurentii, Alamanus. Vault Ayer 6 P9 B5 1480a. Courtesy of The Newberry Library, Chicago (Gift of Edward E. Ayer)

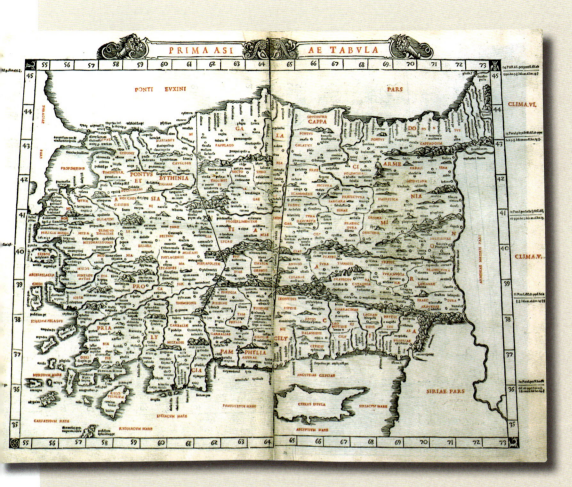

FIGURE 4. Bernardus Sylvanus. *Prima Asiae Tabvla.* [1511]. From *Clavdii Ptolemaei Alexandrini Liber geographiae .... Venetiis per Iacobum Pentium de leucho Anno domini M.D.XI.* The O. J. Sopranos Collection

Absent from the map is any reference to the changing political and cultural geography of the region since Ptolemy's time. Thus it is still Iconium (the classical and Byzantine name for the present-day Turkish city of Konya), Nicaea (Iznik), and Nicomedia (Izmit), and fifty years after the capture of Istanbul by Sultan Mehmed II, the city is still Constantinopolis.

As the limitations of the Ptolemaic maps became increasingly evident, some editors and cartographers sought to remedy the deficiencies of earlier editions either by adding new "modern" maps or by amending the traditional maps to incorporate new information. Prominent among these individuals were Bernardus Sylvanus, whose new edition of Ptolemy was published in Venice in 1511, and Martin Waldseemüller, who prepared the maps for the 1513 Strasbourg edition. In his preface to the text, Sylvanus explains that his intention has been to cast a critical eye at the geographic information in the Ptolemaic world and regional maps, and in a separate chapter he lists the changes that he has made in order to justify "why our maps differ from those drawn by others before us" (quoted in Karrow, *Mapmakers*, p. 524). Since many of the changes involve coastlines and coastal features, it seems highly probable that much of the "new" information was taken from portolan charts (Karrow, *Mapmakers*, pp. 522–24). This influence is perhaps evident in Sylvanus' map of Asia Minor (entitled *Prima Asiae Tabvla*) (fig. 4), where the coast of modern Turkey, particularly the southern Mediterranean coastline, and the islands of Cyprus, Rhodes, Lesbos, and Chios, are much more accurately mapped than in any previous Ptolemaic atlas. However, away from the coastline, while the relief is depicted less monolithically, the classical toponyms and regional divisions are repeated.

Sylvanus was the only editor who attempted to amend Ptolemy's maps, and as such "his maps are ... a curious amalgam of traditional and new geography, and constitute apt symbols of the tension between classical and modern learning that characterized the later Renaissance" (Karrow, *Mapmakers*, p. 522). A different approach to the problem of reconciling "classical and modern learning" was taken by Martin Waldseemüller. The edition of Ptolemy published in Strasbourg by Johann Schott, in 1513, includes a total of twenty entirely new maps by Waldseemüller, *tabulae novae* that are grouped together in a separate section of the atlas with their own title page and preface. In explaining why he has adopted this approach, the editor argues that it is necessary to "confine the Geography of Ptolemy ... so that its antiquity may remain intact," and lest anyone accuse the author of being unaware of the many changes that have occurred with the passage of time, new maps will enable the reader "to inform himself more accurately about modern travel" (quoted in ibid., p. 579).

Among Waldseemüller's *tabulae novae* is what is arguably, at least in the context of early sixteenth-century cartographic knowledge and conventions, the first "modern" map of Turkey. The map displayed in the exhibit European Cartographers and the Ottoman World is actually from a later 1541 Ptolemy edited by Michel de Villeneuve (better known to us as Servetus), but the maps for this edition were copied directly from Waldseemüller. At first glance, this

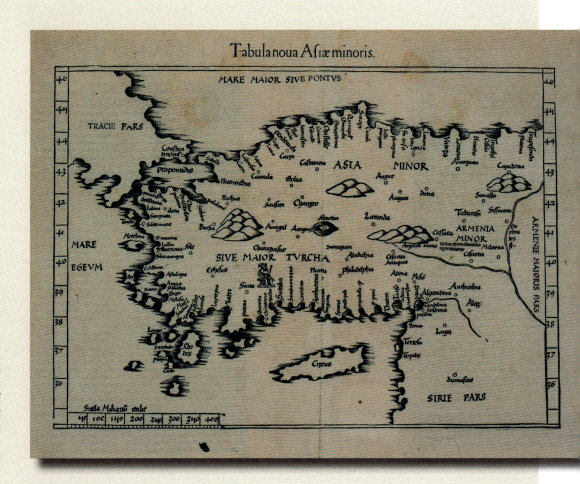

FIGURE 5. Lorenz Fries. *Tabula noua Asiæ minoris.* [1541]. From *Clavdii Ptolemaei Alexandrini geographicae .... Excudebat Gaspar Treschel Viennae M.D.XLI.* The O. J. Sopranos Collection

map, for all its "new" information, is still a highly simplistic representation that retains much of the style and character of earlier Ptolemaic maps; but it is clear that the cartographer has attempted to purge many of the classical toponyms and regional divisions (fig. 5). Relief is depicted somewhat perfunctorily in the form of a few isolated "mountains," while rivers other than the Euphrates and the Orontes have been completely eliminated. The map does add one geographic feature not found on any earlier Ptolemaic map, and that is an inland lake in central Anatolia. More information is presented for places along the coastline (somewhat in the style of a portolan chart) than for the interior, but for all its shortcomings this is the first Ptolemaic map to make a specific reference to sixteenth-century political realities with the inscription "Asia Minor sive Maior Tvrcha." Beneath this inscription is a seated figure (not found on the original 1513 woodcut) that appears to be carrying a staff. What this is intended to symbolize is unclear from the context of the map, but the figure, with its strange clothing and crown, is similar in appearance to those used in sixteenth-century histories printed in Italy and Germany to illustrate the genealogies of Ottoman sultans.

As Norman Thrower has observed, Ptolemaic maps were both the starting point and the model against which advances in geographical knowledge came to be measured (Thrower, *Maps and Civilization*, p. 59). In its sharp distinction between "classical" and "modern" geographical knowledge, Waldseemüller's atlas therefore marks a break from the Ptolemaic tradition. Nearly all subsequent editions follow Waldseemüller's model, clearly distinguishing between *tabulae novae* and the more traditional classical maps, even where these maps appear side by side in the atlas, as in Giacomo Gastaldi's 1548 edition. The gradual weakening of Ptolemy's influence on cartography as the sixteenth century progressed is reflected in Gerardus Mercator's *Tabulae geographicae C. Ptolemei* (1578), which includes only the traditional Ptolemaic maps. By this time, the maps were considered to be strictly of historical value. And by the last quarter of the sixteenth century, in place of Ptolemy's *Geographia*, the great atlases of Ortelius and Mercator had become the standard references and authoritative representations of the modern world.

from the Ptolemaic map, but others were less willing to challenge the classical authorities, even where there were alternative sources of information.[9]

That the Ottomans were fully conversant with these developments in mapmaking is clear from M. Pınar Emiralioğlu's essay on the shaping of Ottoman geographical knowledge during this period (pp. 97–109). She describes a steady flow of intellectuals, artists, and craftsmen to Istanbul in the late fifteenth century, as well as Sultan Mehmed II's well-known interest in classical Greek texts, particularly those on astronomy and cosmography. We know that Mehmed's library contained several richly illustrated manuscript copies of the *Geographia*, and, according to contemporary chroniclers, it was Mehmed's personal dissatisfaction with the quality of the maps that led the sultan to charge George Amirutzes of Trebizond with the preparation of a new, clearer, and more comprehensible world map, one that combined all the information from the regional maps into a single *mappa mundi* (Jardine, *Worldly Goods*, p. 251; Karamustafa, "Maps and Plans," p. 210). As Brotton observes: "The Ottomans were politically and intellectually powerful participants in the early modern world, and their leaders were as compliant and enthusiastic in the patronage of scholarship and artistic production as their Italian counterparts" (Brotton, *Trading Territories*, pp. 97–98).

The flow of ideas, the trade in maps, and the search for patronage that was involved come together in the 1482 *Geographia*, edited by Francesco di Nicolò Berlinghieri.[10] Here we find an atlas, edited by a member of a well-established Florentine family and a prominent figure in the city's humanist circles in the second half of the fifteenth century, that carried a personal dedication to the Ottoman sultan. The story underlying this dedication has been well related by Brotton (*Trading Territories*, pp. 90-95). Frustrated by difficulties in completing the plates for his atlas as a result of the lack of copper engravers skilled in mapmaking, Berlinghieri took the initiative of inscribing manuscript dedications in the front of selected printed copies as a way of soliciting patronage, including one "To Mehmed of the Ottomans, illustrious prince and lord of the throne of God, emperor and merciful lord of all Asia and Greece, I dedicate this work" (quoted in ibid., p. 90). Berlinghieri was somewhat unlucky in his choice of dedicatees, however, a fact that may have further contributed to the delay in printing his work. As Berlinghieri explains in a letter to Sultan Bayezid II which was inserted into the presentation copy taken to Istanbul, the news of Mehmed's death had reached Florence only after he had written the original dedication. In his search for an alternative patron of comparable stature, Berlinghieri turned to Federigo da Montefeltro, Duke of Albino, but unfortunately the duke also died before the final proofs had been corrected. "The fact that Berlinghieri repeatedly attempted to dedicate the *Geographia* to an Ottoman sultan, over and above potential Italian patrons like the Medici family, is powerful testimony to the political weight and cultural authority which emanated from the Ottoman court, an authority which was felt even amongst the scholars of fifteenth-century Florence" (ibid., pp. 94-95).

While Ptolemy's enormous influence on fifteenth-century Renaissance inquiry in general, and mapmaking in particular, has been emphasized, by the beginning of the sixteenth century his ideas and theories had become something of a liability in the face of accumulating geographical knowledge. As Brown aptly puts it, "Ptolemy was both a keystone and a millstone" (*Story of Maps*, p. 74). To many, exhilarated by the new discoveries, the continuing hold of classical cosmography on geographic inquiry was enslaving and frustrating. "Had I Ptolemy, Strabo, Pliny or Salinus here," observed the sixteenth-century Portuguese historian of exploration João de Barros, "I would put them to shame and confusion" (quoted in Livingstone, *Geographical Tradition*, p. 34). This tension between the old learning and the new, between geographical knowledge derived from Greek cosmographical theory and texts, and the knowledge gained from ocean voyaging and overland travel, is one of the defining characteristics of Renaissance cartography (Campbell, *Earliest Printed Maps*, p. 1). As Livingstone (*Geographical Tradition*, pp. 34-35) and O'Sullivan (*Age of Discovery*, p. 3) have suggested, it is perhaps not too fanciful to see the voyages of discovery as a large-scale experiment intended to prove or disprove the geographical concepts transmitted from the classical world. And in a very practical sense, the efforts of cartographers over the next two centuries were directed in no small part to removing the last remaining vestiges of classical geography from their "modern" maps, in favor of "accuratissima" based on real-world observations.

GIACOMO GASTALDI AND THE "NEW" MAP OF ASIA

For most of the sixteenth century, Venice was pre-eminent among Italian city-states in the production of geographical knowledge. Its engravers and publishers dominated the map trade, and perhaps only Lafreri in Rome could match the Venetian ateliers of Camoccio, Pagano, Forlani, and Bertelli for the quality and comprehensiveness of their map holdings (Cosgrove, *Apollo's Eye*, p. 144). Through its far-reaching diplomatic network and its extensive commercial and trading connections, Venice was in a position to act as "a clearing house for reports of geographical discovery at a time when such knowledge was tightly controlled in those European states competing more directly for the spoils of oceanic navigation" (ibid., p. 144). Cosgrove has written extensively about the cosmographic culture of Venice and its global view, and in few other places in the early sixteenth century were the theoretical and intellectual implications of discovery and representation so tightly coupled with the practical and instrumental function of mapmaking in the service of diplomacy and commerce.

Giacomo Gastaldi (ca. 1500-1566) was "cosmographer to the Republic of Venice" and probably the most influential cartographer of the mid-sixteenth century.[11] His activities in Venice encompassed much more than mapmaking, however, and he was regularly commissioned by such agencies as the Magistratura delle Acque (responsible for managing the region's canals, lagoons, and waterways) to design, survey, and engineer public works projects. Little is known about his early life, but by the early 1550s he had produced a considerable body of work including maps for a new edition of Ptolemy, published in Venice in 1548, and a widely admired and much-copied world map (Karrow, *Mapmakers*, pp. 216–49). His official position brought him into contact with the intellectual and political elite of Venice, and a measure of Gastaldi's professional reputation and standing in the city is to be found in two commissions to prepare cartoons and models for a series of large mural maps in the Ducal Palace.[12] Another commission, as we have seen, was the *mappa mundi* requested by "Lord Sultan Selim." Evidence of Gastaldi's continuing interest in the geography of the Ottoman world is to be found in his map of Turkey and Persia, published in 1555 (fig. 6), a map of Asia Minor, [*Il disegno d'geografia moderna della prouincia di Natolia, et Carmania, patria de gli. Sigri. Turchi della casa Ottomana*], printed in Venice in 1564, and other projects for which licensing privileges were apparently sought and granted.[13]

FIGURE 6. Giacomo Gastaldi. *Totivs Illivs regionis qvam hodie Tvrcicam vocant nec non Persiæ regni exactissima descriptio.* Antverpiae apvd Hieronymvm Cock. 1555. Courtesy of the Herzog August Bibliothek, Wolfenbuettel, Germany

Gastaldi's large-scale map of Asia, published between 1559 and 1561 (fig. 7), is a particularly fine example of mid-sixteenth century Venetian cartography and illustrates how far mapping had moved beyond the theoretical framework and classical knowledge obtainable from Ptolemy's *Geographia*. In achieving a synthesis of contemporary cosmographic ideas and "new" geographic knowledge, Gastaldi's map of Asia became the starting point and reference source for later cartographers, whose frequent borrowings and adaptations, often without acknowledgment, further reinforced the map's authority. Thus all the late sixteenth-century and early seventeenth-century maps of the Ottoman world in Asia, including those by Gerard de Jode and Abraham Ortelius, as well as maps of the Ottoman empire from the Mercator-Hondius-Jansson and Blaeu publishing houses, are based on Gastaldi's map and sources. Gastaldi's influence (in terms of cartographic style and geographic content) can still be seen in maps produced well into the seventeenth century, as exemplified in Frederick de Witt's map *Tvrcivm Imperivm* printed in Amsterdam in 1680.

Much of the new information included in Gastaldi's map of Asia was obtained as a result of his association with a small group of Venetian intellectuals, scholars, and public servants, whose meetings constituted something of an informal "cosmographic academy." The discussions of the "academy" served to advance geographic thought

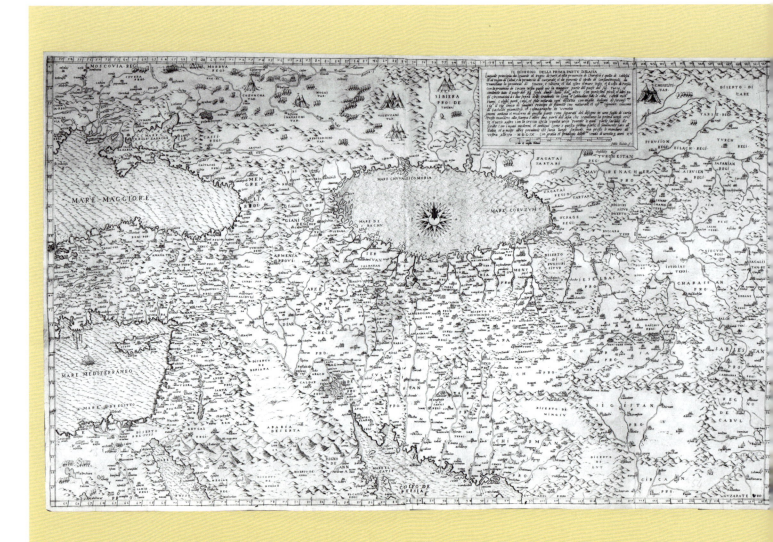

FIGURE 7. Giacomo Gastaldi. (left) *Il disegno della prima parte del A*
Venetia [Venice] 1559 (Novacco 4F 373); and (r
Il disegno della seconda parte dell'A

and practice in a city where global knowledge was regarded as key to its continued commercial and diplomatic success (Cosgrove, *Apollo's Eye*, pp. 143–44). In particular, Gastaldi was a close friend of Giovanni Battista Ramusio, secretary to the Venetian Senate and, from 1553, to the powerful Council of Ten which ruled the city-state. We know that Ramusio entrusted Gastaldi with the instruction of his son in cosmography, and it seems likely that it was his friendship with Ramusio that helped secure the commissions for the mural maps in the Ducal Palace (Karrow, *Mapmakers*, p. 216). Gastaldi and Ramusio were also members of the Accademia della Fama, which, in the 1550s, sought to renew the city's civic and material fabric in the face of changing political and commercial circumstances (Cosgrove, *Apollo's Eye*, p. 146).

Here, clearly, was the basis for collaboration. Ramusio's official position gave him unrivaled access to the latest geographical information reaching Venice, and he seems to have shared his knowledge and sources with Gastaldi from a quite early date. Ramusio's singular scholarly achievement was the collection and editing of travel narratives, and his massive three-volume *Delle Navigationi et Viaggi* was published in Venice between 1550 and 1559.[14] Almost certainly the anonymous woodcut maps that accompany the text were contributed by Gastaldi (fig. 8).

…etia [Venice] 1561 (Novacco 4F 386). These form the first two parts of
…aldi's three-part map of Asia. Courtesy of The Newberry
…ary, Chicago (Franco Novacco Map Collection)

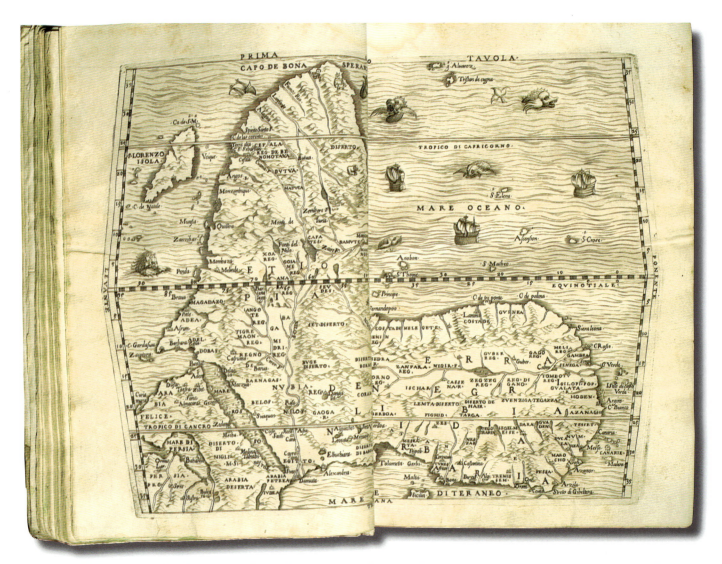

FIGURE 8. [Giacomo Gastaldi]. [*Africa*]. 1563. From [Giovanni Battista Ramusio], *Delle Navigationi et Viaggi Raccolto da M. Gio. Batt. Ramvsio & con molti vaghi discorsi* .... Primo volume, & Terza editione. Venetia [Venice]: Stamperia de Givnti. M.D.LXIII. Courtesy of The University of Chicago Library, Special Collections Research Center

Ramusio's correspondence reveals the gradual evolution of this project, from its initial conception in the course of informal conversations with friends and close associates, to the monumental undertaking that absorbed his energies over nearly thirty years (Howard, "Status of the Oriental Traveller," pp. 37–38). During this period, Ramusio used his network of friends and political connections to acquire geographical texts and travel narratives. He translated those in Latin, Greek, French, Spanish, and Portuguese into the Tuscany dialect that was emerging as the preferred literary form of Italian and added his own commentary addressing a wide range of general geographical questions, such as the source of the annual floods of the Nile. The whole enterprise had a cartographic agenda. This is stated quite explicitly by Ramusio in the introduction to the first volume, where he writes that there is no more urgent task than to provide the materials and information needed by cartographers to correct the deficiencies of Ptolemy and thereby remove the errors about the world inherited from Antiquity (Parks, "Contents and Sources," p. 282).

In terms of the wealth of material collected, no other compilation could match Ramusio's achievement: here, in a single collection, were reproduced nearly all the major travel narratives written before the mid-sixteenth century, many of which had not been previously published. The accompanying essay on Abu al-Fida illustrates the scope and breadth of Ramusio's undertaking, as well as its specific cartographic application. Thus Ramusio includes a table of latitudes and longitudes taken from the geography of Abu al-Fida (almost certainly provided to Ramusio by the French oriental scholar and linguist Guillaume Postel) to enable mapmakers to locate the cities in Asia described by

FIGURE 9. [*World Map*]. From *Tarih-i Hind-i Garbi* [*History of the India of the West*]. Anonymous Ottoman manuscript, ca. 1600. This world map (oriented with north at the bottom) is based on Giacomo Gastaldi's *Carta marina nova tabvla*, which appeared in *La geografia di Clavdio Ptolemeo Alessandrino ...*, printed in Venice by G. B. Pedrezano, 1548. Ayer MS 612. Courtesy of The Newberry Library, Chicago (Gift of Edward E. Ayer)

Marco Polo. Similarly, Tibbetts (*Arabia in Early Maps*, p. 21) has documented the way in which Gastaldi's mapping of the Arabian peninsula incorporates information that could only have come from texts made available to him by Ramusio.[15] Of course it would be quite wrong to assume that this information was always correct, but as Tibbetts observes, Ramusio's texts and Gastaldi's maps largely defined cartographic knowledge of Arabia for the next century and a half. "To practically all cosmographers, cartographers and historians of discovery who wrote in the late sixteenth and early seventeenth century, Ramusio was either the logical starting point for their work or their most reliable reference" (Lach, *Asia*, p. 208).

Alongside the copy of Ramusio's *Navigationi et Viaggi* displayed in the exhibit is a late sixteenth-century Ottoman manuscript, *Tarih-i Hind-i Garbi* [*History of the India of the West*], which is itself a remarkable compilation of geographical knowledge about the Americas. Covering the first six decades of European contact, from the voyages of Columbus and Magellan to the conquests of Cortes and Pizarro, with additional information on natural history, physical geography, and anthropology, the unknown author of the *Tarih-i Hind-i Garbi* translates brief passages from published accounts of the Americas and relates this new knowledge to the information appearing in more traditional Islamic geographies (Goodrich, *Ottoman Turks*). Although the *Tarih-i Hind-i Garbi* does not appear to have been compiled with the same explicit mapping agenda that Ramusio had in mind for the *Navigationi et Viaggi*, the manuscript does include a series of world maps, one of which is a copy of a map prepared by Gastaldi for the edition of

Ptolemy published in Venice in 1548 (fig. 9). In a number of ways, therefore, the manuscript demonstrates once again just how familiar the Ottomans were with the geographical knowledge and texts being produced elsewhere in Europe. Indeed, it is not inconceivable that Ramusio was one of the sources used by the author of the *Tarih-i Hind-i Garbi*.[16] That there was considerable interest in this subject is evident from the number of copies of the manuscript that have survived from the late sixteenth and seventeenth centuries.[17] Moreover, in the early eighteenth century, the *Tarih-i Hind-i Garbi* was the fourth book selected for publication by the first Ottoman press, and the first with illustrations, a further indication of its long-term relevance to Ottoman geographical thinking (Watson, "Ibrahim Müterferrika"). While the subject matter of *Tarih-i Hind-i Garbi* is unusual among known Ottoman manuscripts, and while its impact and reach was certainly limited by comparison with the printed geographical texts circulating in western Europe, it is clear that Ottoman geographies of the sixteenth century were every bit as global in their vision, scope, and information as those being produced elsewhere in Europe.

ABRAHAM ORTELIUS' *TVRCICI IMPERII DESCRIPTIO*

By the beginning of the seventeenth century, the maps and atlases of Abraham Ortelius (1527–1598) and Gerardus Mercator (1512–1594) had thoroughly superseded Ptolemy's *Geographia* as the new authoritative image of the world. These cartographers derived much of their information from sources such as Ramusio and were indebted to the more systematic approach of Gastaldi, but they established a basic organizational framework for presenting geographical information that was followed by other mapmakers for much of the seventeenth century. Thus we find the same cartographic conventions and geographic content — framing, lettering, decorated cartouche, regional toponyms, representation of topography and settlement — in the work of Willem and Joan Blaeu, who, along with the Mercator-Hondius-Jansson publishing house, dominated map and atlas production in the first half of the seventeenth century.

This new "cartographic language" is well illustrated in maps of the Ottoman empire by Gerard de Jode, Abraham Ortelius, and Frederick de Witt (figs. 10–12). Beginning with the 1606 edition prepared by Jodocus Hondius, Mercator's world atlas also included a map of the Ottoman empire (entitled *Turcici Imperii Imago*), which, relying on the same sources, is not surprisingly a reiteration of the same geography in all but the most minor details (fig. 13). A close reading of these maps also illustrates the persistence of geographic information once it had found its way onto the map. Particularly noteworthy in this regard is the naming and distinctive (albeit inaccurate) configurations of the "Mare de Bachv ol. Caspivm Mare..." (Caspian Sea), "Mare el Catif ol. Sinvs Persicvs" (Persian Gulf), and "Mare de Mecca olim sinvs Arabicvs" (Red Sea) as drawn in Ortelius' map (*Tvrcici Imperii Descriptio*) and that of de Witt (*Tvrcicvm Imperivm*), even though these maps were printed nearly a century apart.

To the modern eye it is perhaps surprising that the world view depicted in these maps finds little need to deal cartographically with political territoriality or geographical hierarchies. The geography of the Ottoman empire in maps from the first half of the seventeenth century, for example, is remarkably undifferentiated. Place names are randomly located with little attention or consideration given to rank, size, or significance. Regional names often seem arbitrarily selected and placed to fill the available space. But perhaps most striking is the lack of attention given to political boundaries.

The neglect of political information about the Ottoman empire on these maps (as on other regional maps from this period) in favor of topographic and toponymic information suggests a very different way of conceptualizing political space at this time, one in which boundaries and territories were not yet seen as central to the political order. As Akerman has observed ("Structuring of Political Territory"), sovereignty in Europe in the late sixteenth and early seventeenth centuries — although obviously contested — was still fundamentally seen as a matter of personal allegiance and dynastic influence. And what the sovereign rules is not so much a territory as a people; in many cases this "sovereignty" overarches communities with different forms of governance and religion. In many cases there was a lack of geographical contiguity with spatially separated communities owing allegiance to the same overlord. In such circumstances it was not unusual for duchies and counties to be exchanged fairly regularly in the course of peace treaties, customs agreements, and marriage arrangements. This was a rather different construction of political space, where boundaries were fluid and non-demarcated on the ground, more easily described, perhaps, than mapped. It finds expression cartographically in the absence of borders and the sort of clearly differentiated and sharply bounded political territories that were to become the standard vocabulary of maps later in the century.

In viewing these maps, it is important to recall that, although often printed and sold separately as individual sheets, they were for the most part conceived as part of a larger work. The model for this was Abraham Ortelius's *Theatrum Orbis Terrarum*, the first edition of which appeared in 1570. As Cosgrove has observed (*Apollo's Eye*, p. 130), while the *Theatrum* drew its inspiration from Ptolemy's *Geographia*, from the popular cosmographies of Hartmann Schedel and Sebastian Münster, and from the ad hoc collections of printed maps bound together and sold by Bertelli and Lafreri, it was intended to hold up a mirror to the whole earth. Ortelius's immediate achievement lay in the systematic organization of geographical information, with maps arranged by continent and region, and in the re-engraving of the best maps available to a uniform size and format. But his purpose was more broadly imagined, a unifying humanistic vision of the globe, scientifically mapped to disclose "the secrets of a new world" and thereby reveal its underlying order and harmony. The popular appeal of the *Theatrum* can be judged by the frequency of reprintings (four in the first year of its publication alone and a total of twenty-four in Ortelius' lifetime) and the number of translations. In its total encompassing vision of the globe it was matched only by Mercator's

FIGURE 10. Gerard de Jode. *Tvrcia Tvrcicive Imperii seu Solij mannorum regni pleraque pars, nunc recens summa fide ac industria elucubrata.* 1579. From *Specvlvm Orbis Terrarvm.* Antwerp. The O. J. Sopranos Collection

FIGURE 11. Abraham Ortelius. *Tvrcici Imperii Descriptio.* [1579]. From *Theatrum Orbis Terrarum.* [Antwerp], 1602.
The O. J. Sopranos Collection

atlas which appeared some twenty-five years later, while its lineage and influence is clear in the similar undertakings of Jodocus and Henricus Hondius, Jan Jansson, and the Blaeu family in The Netherlands, and of the Homann publishing house in Nuremberg, helping to pave the way for what Bagrow (*History of Cartography*, p. 179) has called "the century of atlases."

Many of these atlases found their way into the Ottoman world, and the continued interest in geography as both an intellectual and practical undertaking is evident in translations into Ottoman Turkish of Mercator's *Atlas minor* (by the well-known scholar Katib Çelebi in A.H. 1064/1065 [A.D. 1653/1655]) and of Joan Blaeu's *Atlas maior* (by Ebu Bekir ibn Behram el-Dimaşki, completed between A.H. 1086 and 1096 [A.D. 1675–1685]) (Karamustafa, "Maps and Plans," p. 218). Further evidence of the practical interest in mapping in the Ottoman world in the seventeenth century is to be found in the writing of the Turkish traveler and author Evliya Çelebi, who includes chart makers and compass makers in his list of Istanbul guilds. "The map-makers are but fifteen in eight shops. They are deeply versed in all kinds of sciences, and possess different languages, particularly the Latin, in which they read the geographical works *Atlas minor* and *Mappemonde*. They lay down in their drawings the seas, rivers and mountains of the whole world, and sell their works to sailors and navigators" (Evliya Çelebi, quoted in Soucek, "Islamic Charting," p. 284).

FIGURE 12. Frederick de Witt. *Tvrcicvm Imperivm*. From *Atlas maior*. Amsterdam, 1680[?]. The O. J. Sopranos Collection

Karrow (*Mapmakers*, p. 9) makes the important point that Ortelius' *Theatrum* was much more than a commercial success, and the same may be said of the great atlases of the seventeenth century. They were prized as objects to be collected, displayed, and admired, as much as for the geographical knowledge they contained. Accordingly, maps and atlases were increasingly embellished with ornate cartouches, baroque frontispieces with symbolic personifications of the continents, and surrounded by additional images of peoples, cities, monuments, historical events, and natural flora and fauna. Cosgrove (*Apollo's Eye*, p. 130) puts it slightly differently, suggesting that "Ortelius's work encouraged the idea of private, vicarious enjoyment of geographic discovery ...; [in these images] the individual could master the globe at a single glance." In his dedication of a twelve-volume edition of the *Atlas maior* to Louis XIV, Joan Blaeu describes geography as "the eye and the light of history" such that "maps enable us to contemplate at home and right before our eyes things that are farthest away" (quoted in Livingstone, *Geographical Tradition*, p. 98). Here, perhaps, is as good an assessment as any of the changing nature of geographic thought and cartographic representation in the latter half of the sixteenth and the first half of the seventeenth centuries, what Livingstone (ibid., pp. 98–99) describes as the triumph of representational modes of thinking, such that picturing, or mapping, or modeling the world comes to be seen as the only reliable way of knowing it.

FIGURE 13. [Henricus Hondius]. *Turcici Imperii Imago.* From *Atlas sive Cosmographicae meditationes de fabrica mvndi et fabricati figvra. Primum à Gerardo Mercatore inchoatae, deinde a Iudoco Hondio Piae memoriae ... Sumptibus & typis aeneis Henrici Hondij.* Amsterdam, 1630. Vault Oversize Ayer 135 .M5 1630. Courtesy of The Newberry Library, Chicago

ENLIGHTENED FRENCH CARTOGRAPHY AND THE MAPPING OF THE OTTOMAN EMPIRE[18]

In the first half of the seventeenth century, French cartography lagged far behind that of the Dutch, not only in map and atlas production, but also in such related fields as navigation, applied mathematics, and instrument making (Konvitz, *Cartography in France*). There was no comparable "French" Ortelius, and most of the maps and atlases sold in Paris by publishers such as Melchior Tavernier were French editions of the great Mercator-Hondius and Blaeu atlases (Pastoureau, "French School Atlases"). By the end of the seventeenth century, however, the situation had been completely reversed, and it was French mapmakers who were the dominant force in European cartography. Their maps drew praise from contemporaries for setting new standards of accuracy and applying scientific principles to mapmaking. The French cartographer Nicolas Sanson (1600–1677) had achieved almost cult status by the end of the seventeenth century, so frequently were his maps and geographical tables being copied and imitated

(Pastoureau, *Les Sansons*). The Dutch, in particular, appropriated Sanson's work and name with abandon, most notably the publisher Pieter Mortier, who pirated an entire edition of the *Atlas Nouveau*, the maps in the version published in Amsterdam in 1696 bearing the counterfeit imprint of Alexis-Hubert Jaillot, Sanson's publisher in Paris.[19] The widespread practice of copying and reprinting maps was often at odds with the professed goals of geographical accuracy. An early eighteenth-century reviewer of Herman Moll's *Atlas Geographicus*, for example, while praising the high quality of the engravings (exemplified in the map of the Turkish empire), berated Moll for uncritically reproducing information from Sanson's maps, commenting that "If something of this Kind had been done before, there had probably been a Stop put, ere now, to that Swarm of spurious Maps that are abroad" (John Green, *The Construction of Maps and Globes*. London, 1717, quoted in Reinhartz, *Cartographer and Literati*, p. 29).

Sanson's concern with organizing and mapping geographical information "scientifically" is repeated in the approach of Guillaume de L'Isle (1675-1726) and Jean Baptiste d'Anville (1697-1782). But the standing of French cartography during this period was further advanced by the national map survey of France, undertaken between 1681 and 1744 under the direction of the Cassini family. It was the successful completion of this project as much as the scholarship of Sanson, de L'Isle, and d'Anville that transformed mapmaking and the contexts in which maps were used (Konvitz, *Cartography in France*, p. 1). While these developments in French cartography affected mapmaking generally, the new ways of conceptualizing and organizing political space had far-reaching implications for the mapping of the Ottoman empire and for the ways in which Europeans came to imagine and visualize Ottoman territories in Europe and Asia.

In the exhibit European Cartographers and the Ottoman World, the *Carte de l'Empire des Tvrcs ...*, published in 1664 by Sanson's son-in-law Pierre du Val; Guillaume de L'Isle's *Carte de la Turquie de l'Arabie et de la Perse ...*, as copied by the Dutch publishers Jean Cóvens and Corneille Mortier for a 1745 atlas published in Amsterdam; and Herman Moll's *The Turkish Empire in Europe, Asia and Africa ...* (1720), illustrate the achievements and influence of French cartography during this period (figs. 14-16). These maps, in contrast to those of Gastaldi, Ortelius, Mercator, and Blaeu, employ systems of markers and colors in strikingly visual ways to map political territory and boundaries, no matter how dubious their relationship to the situation on the ground. Sanson was the first cartographer to do this in a systematic way, delineating various hierarchies of boundaries with gradations of dotted or dashed lines, but by the end of the seventeenth century this had become standard practice for all regional maps and large-format world atlases (Akerman, "Structuring of Political Territory," p. 141).

Sanson's biographer describes him as "par excellence la pédagogue de la nomenclature" (Pastoureau, *Nicolas Sanson d'Abbeville*, p. 24). Certainly his innovative use of tables as a way of organizing geographical information (repeatedly dividing and subdividing the world) situates Sanson's methods within the wider intellectual and scientific search for order and explanation that marks the French Enlightenment. But as Akerman suggests ("Structuring of Political Territory," pp. 140-41), Sanson's "obsession with spatial hierarchies" cannot be set apart from the efforts by the French crown in the second half of the seventeenth century to strengthen the authority of the central administration and regularize its relationship with the regions. The particular concern for political order and hierarchies is often embedded in the title of the map. The map of the Ottoman empire in the 1689 edition of Sanson's *Atlas Nouveau*, presented to the French Dauphin, for example, is entitled *Estats de l'Empire du Grand Seigneur des Tvrcs en Europe, en Asie, et en Afrique divisé en touts ses Beglerbeglicz, ou Gouvernements ou sont aussi remarqués les Estats qui luy sont Tributaires* (fig. 17). The map is accompanied by a series of geographical tables that further subdivide the territories, classifying them from the largest to the smallest administrative unit (fig. 18), and on occasions providing additional notes about their "Christian" and "Turkish" populations. As Pastoureau has noted, such practices, combined with Sanson's insistence on consistency in the formatting and appearance of all regional maps, ensured that the vision of the world he provided was familiar and reassuring, "since all these territories were carefully divided by diagrammatic borders, giving the impression of spaces perfectly controlled intellectually" (Pastoureau, "French School Atlases," pp. 116-17).

While Sanson's maps were applauded for their accuracy, his work, like that of de L'Isle and d'Anville, remained essentially that of the *géographe de la cabinet*. Their maps were compiled from a careful comparison of existing maps, charts, and other geographical materials, supplemented by the observations and reports of hopefully "informed" travelers, missionaries, and government agents.[20] D'Anville in particular gained a reputation for scrupulous attention to detail, critically comparing a wide range of sources, maintaining an extensive correspondence with informants (in the process accumulating an unrivalled personal collection of nearly nine thousand maps and geographical texts), and correcting and reissuing maps as new information became available (Konvitz, *Cartography in France*, pp. 33–34). For each new or revised map, d'Anville published a *mémoire* critically evaluating the sources used in preparing the map. D'Anville's *mémoire* accompanying the 1776 map of the Persian Gulf, for example, lists among his sources early Arab geographers (including al-Idrisi and Abu al-Fida), the seventeenth-century Ottoman geographer Katib Çelebi, and the narratives of European travelers such as Jean de Thévenot.

French cartographers, therefore, like the earlier humanist mapmakers of the fifteenth and sixteenth centuries, were fully conversant with historical sources, but what distinguishes their work, in keeping with the intellectual spirit of the French Enlightenment, is the weight placed on direct observation and measurement as the basis for scientific advancement. Herman Moll makes the point explicitly in his preface to *The Compleat Geographer*: "As the Knowledge of Foreign Countries is a Science that no Man of either Learning or Business can excusably be without, so there is no certain way of attaining it but by consulting the Travellers that have been upon the Spot" (Moll 1709,

FIGURE 14. Pierre du Val. *Carte de l'Empire des Tvrcs et de les contins. From Le Monde, ou, La Geographie universelle contenent les descriptions, les cartes & le blazon de principaux pays du monde.* Paris, 1664. The O. J. Sopranos Collection

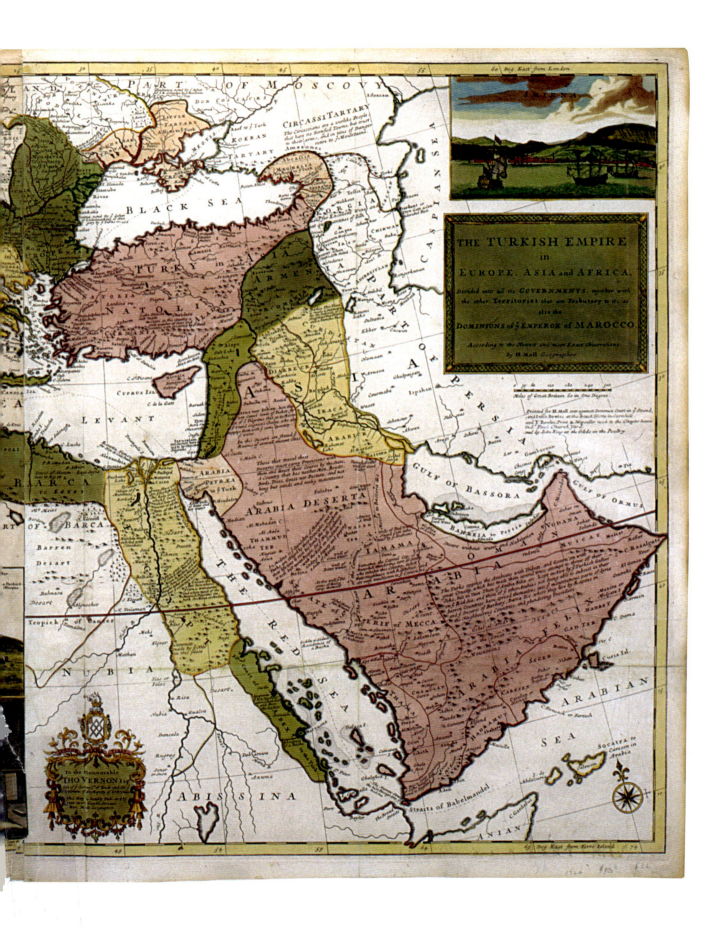

SMYRNA

THE TURKISH EMPIRE
in
EUROPE, ASIA and AFRICA,
Divided into all its GOVERNMENTS, together with
the other Territories that are Tributary to it, as
also the
DOMINIONS of ye EMPEROR of MAROCCO,
According to the Newest and most Exact Observations;
By H Moll Geographer

Miles of Great Britain, 60 in One Degree

PART OF MOSCOVY

CIRCASSITARTARY

DON COSACKS

BLACK SEA

CASPIAN SEA

GEORGIA

CIRCASSITARTARY
The Circassians are a warlike People
that have no Fortified Towns, but trust
to their own in time of Danger
retire to ye Mountains.
Amazons

TURKY in ASIA

NATOLIA

ARMENIA

PART OF PERSIA

DIARBECK

CYPRUS ISL.

LEVANT

IRACA

ASIA

ARABIA
PETRAEA

Those that travel these
Deserts must carry Provisions
and also their Course by the Stars
A Country that has neither Men, Beasts,
Birds, Trees, Grass nor Pasture, but
hang but sands and rocky mountains

ARABIA DESERTA

GULF OF BASSORA

GULF OF ORMUS

BARCA
TO EGYPT

OF BARCA

Barren

Desert

NUBIA

THE

EGYPT

THAMMUD

IAMAMA

ARABIAN

OMAN

MUSCAT

SERIF of MECCA

ARABIA

ARABIA FELIX

THE RED SEA

NUBIA

Tropick of Cancer

SEA

HADRAMUT

Socatra to
Caresm in
Arabia

ABISSINA

ANIAN

Straits of Babelmandel

To the Honourable
THO VERNON Esqr

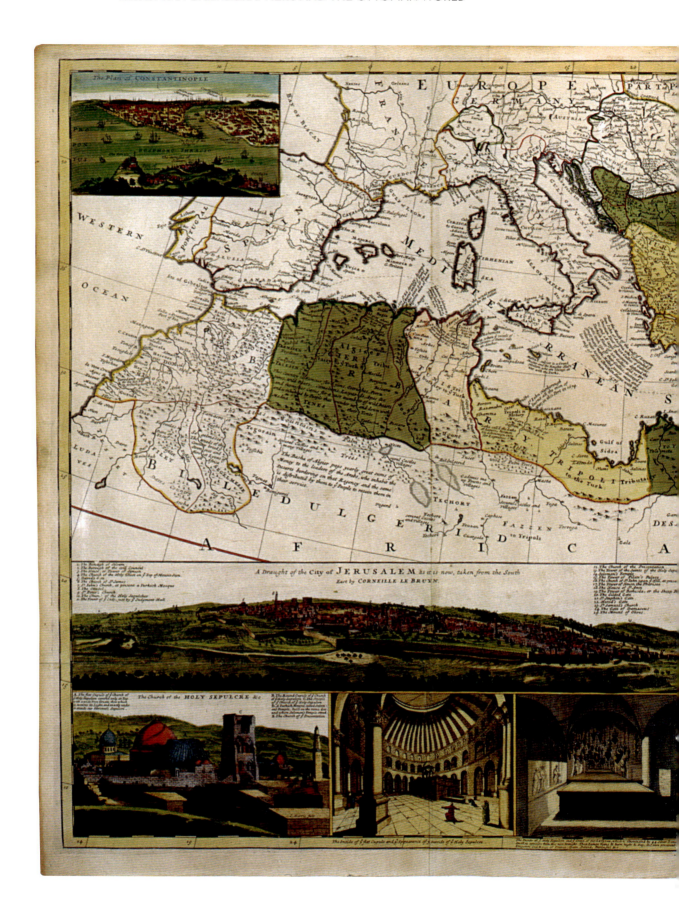

Figure 15. Herman Moll. *The Turkish Empire in Europe, Asia and Africa, Dividid into all its Governments, together with the other Territories that are Tributary to it, as also the Dominions of ye Emperor of Marocco. According to the Newest and most Exact Observations.* London, 1720. The O. J. Sopranos Collection

FIGURE 16. Guillaume de L'Isle. *Carte de la Turquie de l'Arabie et de la Perse. Dressée sur les Memoires les plus recens rectifiez par les Observations de M.rs de l'Academie Roy.le des Sciences.* Amsterdam: Chez Iean Cóvens et Corneille Mortier, 1745. The O. J. Sopranos Collection

FIGURE 17. Nicolas Sanson. *Estats de l'Empire du Grand Seigneur des Turcs en Europe, en Asie, et en Afrique divisé en touts ses Beglerbeglicz, ou Gouvernements ou sont aussi remarqués les Estats qui luy sont Tributaires. Dressé sur les plus nouvelles relations ... Par le Sr. Sanson, Geographe Ordinaire de Roy. From a Dutch counterfeit edition of Atlas Nouveau, Contenant Toutes les Parties du Monde ... (Paris [i.e., Amsterdam]: H. Jaillot [i.e., Pierre Mortier], 1692 [i.e., 1695w]. Vault Oversize Ayer 135 .S19 1692 pl. [94]. Courtesy of The Newberry Library, Chicago*

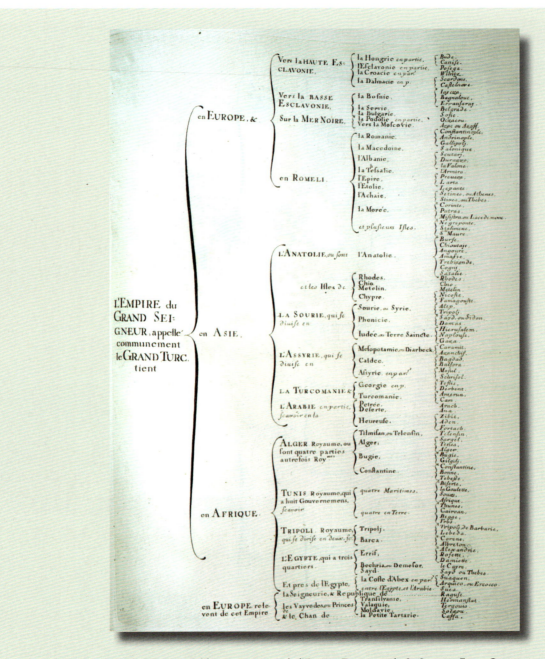

FIGURE 18. Nicolas Sanson. *Tables ou Divisions de l'Empire Turc ... par le S*. *Sanson.* From *Cartes generales de toutes les parties du monde ...*, Volume 2. Paris: P. Mariette, 1658.
Courtesy of The Newberry Library, Chicago

quoted in Reinhartz, *Cartographer and Literati*, p. 39). The close connection between overseas travel, direct observation, and the scientific collection and representation of geographic information evident in seventeenth-century cartography is captured in a project initiated by Robert Boyle (1627–1691), better known for his pioneering work in the fields of chemistry and physics. Toward the end of his life, Boyle began work on a manual for those traveling to China, India, Turkey, southeast Asia, and the New World that would provide clear and consistent guidelines for collecting and recording geographical information (Livingstone, *Geographical Tradition*, p. 102). Writing of the advances in knowledge achieved through the travels of "Gentlemen, Seamen, and others," he observes that "the grea[t] Disadvantage many Ingenious Men are at in their Travels, by reason they know not before-hand what things they are to inform themselves of in every Country they come to, or by what Method they may make Enquiries about things to be known there, I thought it would not be unacceptable to such, to have Directions in General, relating to ... their Particular Countries" (Boyle 1692, quoted in Livingstone, *Geographical Tradition*, p. 103). Boyle's guidelines reveal the underlying preoccupation of geographers and cartographers during the Enlightenment period, along with their contemporaries in other sciences, to proceed in a more rational way with the collection, classification, and representation of geographic data, and anticipates the more scientific expeditions (such as that of Carsten Niebuhr and the Royal Danish Expedition to Arabia) that proliferated in the eighteenth century (ibid., pp. 125–26).

The concern for discovering order in the world and the search for accuracy in the reporting and mapping of geographical information situates the work of Sanson, de L'Isle, d'Anville, and other cartographers of the late seventeenth and eighteenth centuries in the wider intellectual and scientific currents of Enlightenment thought. However, it is necessary to recall Harley's observation that maps are not simply a mirror of the world, but active agents of social and political change: "whether a map is produced under the banner of cartographic science ... or whether it is an overt propaganda exercise, it cannot escape involvement in the processes by which power is deployed" (Harley, "Silences and Secrecy," p. 279). And developments in French cartography in the seventeenth century are clearly connected to both the strengthening of the power and authority of the central administration and to the reshaping of ideas about political territory.

In mid-seventeenth-century France, growing factionalism and local insurrections, a consequence in part of the social and economic dislocation following years of debilitating wars with the Habsburg powers of Spain and Austria, coupled with internal religious schisms, seriously threatened the crown's authority. To ministers of the crown such as Jean Claude Colbert (1619–1683), reversing this situation and revitalizing French economic activity required sweeping administrative reforms and a centralization of power. Mapping was seen as central to that undertaking. Thus Sanson, in his position as *géographe de roi*, was entrusted by Colbert with responsibility for collecting accurate and detailed maps of each province. Where none existed, the crown's agents were to provide Sanson with the information needed for new maps. All aspects of French economic activity and cultural life were to be covered, but Colbert's directions were explicit with respect to mapping the array of military, judicial, fiscal, and ecclesiastical units through which France was governed (Konvitz, *Cartography in France*). It quickly became clear that the available maps lacked the level of accuracy and detail required for the administrative and fiscal reforms that Colbert had in mind. From this need emerged the national map survey of France, based on geodetic surveying and direct measurement in the field. This is not the place to describe the difficulties and challenges that French cartographers encountered in completing the survey, and as Konvitz observes (ibid., p. 8), those who launched the project "perhaps underestimated the effort, time, and money this venture required." But the accomplishments of the French in the practical application of mathematics to surveying, and the successful printing, in 1744, of an eighteen-sheet map of the country based entirely on triangulation, enlarged the scope of cartography and the power of the state in ways that other nations quickly emulated.

"TO CONCLUDE EUROPEAN GEOGRAPHY"[21]

It is perhaps not surprising that the ideas, concerns, and projects of the Enlightenment, often mediated in seen and unseen ways by the needs and interests of the state, should find such clear expression in French cartography. In the process, the emerging European interest in boundaries as a way of ordering and controlling political space came to be projected, quite literally, onto other regions.

Nowhere did this task appear more urgent than in the mapping of the uncertain and shifting boundaries of the Ottoman empire in southeastern Europe. As early as 1671, French cartographers were directed to prepare a map of the border area between the Ottoman empire and its neighbors so that the evolving struggle for political control in southeastern Europe and the shifting fortunes of such territories as Hungary and Wallachia, Slovenia and Croatia, could be monitored more closely in Paris. But, as Wolff notes, for all the claims of "accuratissima" made by the cartographers, the maps they produced were never free from ideological considerations. Strong anti-Habsburg sentiment in France, for example, is reflected in the maps of early eighteenth-century French cartographers who were much more likely than their English and Dutch counterparts to show an "independent" Hungary in the coloring and titling of their maps, despite the complexity of the situation on the ground and the fact that, under the Treaty of Karlowitz (1699), the Ottoman sultan had surrendered control over Hungary to the Habsburgs (Wolff, *Inventing Eastern Europe*, pp. 150–58).[22] The vexed problem of how to represent Hungary cartographically was still troubling Robert de Vaugondy nearly fifty years later when he criticized de L'Isle's 1700 map of Europe "for having ... let Hungary be enveloped in the estates of the Turk in Europe, for that skilful geographer well knew that it was not part of that empire. One must attribute these faults, or rather these light inadvertencies ... to the great occupations that we have, and that do not permit us to verify these maps, accordingly as they are colored" (Robert de Vaugondy 1754, quoted in Wolff, *Inventing Eastern Europe*, p. 150).

Guillaume de L'Isle's *Carte particuliere de la Hongrie, de la Transilvanie, de la Croatie, et de la Sclavonie, Dressée sur les Observations de M*[r]*. le Comte Marsilli et sur plusieurs autre Memoires*, printed in Paris in 1717, provides a fascinating glimpse into the mapping of these borderlands and the function of Enlightenment cartography in the service of the state (fig. 19). As noted by Krokar, this is one of the first European maps to show the course of the Danube accurately, and it was based on surveys carried out under Habsburg auspices according to methods pioneered by Cassini in France (Krokar, *Ottoman Presence*, p. 34). The fieldwork had been conducted by Count Luigi Ferdinando Marsigli, an officer in the Habsburg army, assisted by a German surveyor and draughtsman, Johann Müller, during the campaigns against the Ottomans that preceded the Treaty of Karlowitz.[23] The treaty itself created joint border commissions to demarcate clear boundaries between the domains of the sultan and the victorious powers of the Habsburg-led Holy League, and expressly committed the signatory powers to adherence to the concept of territorial integrity (Abou-el-Haj, "Formal Closure," p. 467). As Konvitz notes, evolving Enlightenment ideas about the link between identity and a clearly bounded territory, a concept that was to become the basis of the modern nation-state, and the state's desire to rationalize borders and resolve contentious boundary issues through mapping, were mutually reinforcing tendencies (Konvitz, *Cartography in France*, p. 32). But the Treaty of Karlowitz appears to mark the first time that these ideas were formally incorporated into international treaty making (Abou-el-Haj, "Formal Closure," p. 467). Marsigli served as a technical adviser to the Habsburg delegation and was subsequently appointed as the Habsburg boundary commissioner charged with demarcating the new frontier on the ground. With his Ottoman counterpart, Marsigli spent the better part of two years tracing the new boundary, including, as specified in the treaty, supervising the construction of cairns and the digging of ditches to identify the frontier wherever it did not follow "natural" features (Stoye, *Marsigli's Europe*, pp. 175–77). Müller produced a number of maps of the border regions, including a general map of the entire frontier presented to Emperor Leopold of Austria, but these had a very restricted circulation (Krokar, *Ottoman Presence*, p. 38).

How this information eventually found its way into the hands of French cartographers is a timely reminder that the production of maps and the dissemination of geographic knowledge can be shaped by personal idiosyncrasies and allegiances as much as by state patronage and wider intellectual currents. Thus early in the War of the Spanish Succession (1702–1714) between the French and an anti-French alliance led by the English, Dutch, and Austrians, Marsigli was court-martialed and cashiered for his role in surrendering the poorly provisioned fortress of Breibach, on the Rhine frontier, to the French. When appeals to his former patron, Emperor Leopold, for reinstatement proved unsuccessful, Marsigli retired to his home in Italy and later made his way to Paris where he was received at court, met with leading French scientists, and became involved in the activities of the newly established Société Royale des Sciences de Montpellier (Stoye, *Marsigli's Europe*).

Wolff's account of the ways whereby the lands between the Ottoman empire and adjacent states came to be studied, mapped, and imagined in western Europe is particularly helpful in illuminating the role of French cartography in this process (Wolff, *Inventing Eastern Europe*). In identifying cartography with the spirit of the Enlightenment, he writes, "the light of cartography was implicitly related to the light of civilization, for Eastern Europe was often described in the eighteenth century as emerging from darkness, *tenebras*" (ibid., p. 149). The claims and views expressed by French cartographers are quite revealing in this regard. According to Robert de Vaugondy, the mapping of the "lost lands" of Europe according to more exacting scientific standards was the special responsibility of French cartography. In the foreword to his 1756 *Atlas maior* he observes that "the beginning of our century must be regarded as the epoch of a general renewal of Geography in France, and, so to say, in all the other lands of Europe, to which it seems this kingdom has been handed the key" (de Vaugondy, quoted in Wolff, *Inventing Eastern Europe*,

FIGURE 19. Guillaume de L'Isle. *Carte particuliere de la Hongrie, de la Transilvanie, de la Croatie, et de la Sclavonie, dressée sur les Observations de M^r. le Comte Marsilli et sur plusieurs autre Memoires.* Paris, 1717. Sack Map 4f G6500 1717 .L5.
Courtesy of The Newberry Library, Chicago (John Gabriel Sack Map Collection)

p. 193). That this mapping project extended to those "lost lands" of Europe under Ottoman control is evident in the frustration expressed by de Vaugondy in the lack of access to these lands for purposes of surveying and mapping. "We would have wished to be able to conclude [*terminer*] European geography with more speed and success; but the approach to these states is difficult for enlightened people [*gens éclaires*], and does not permit one to ever hope for sufficient lights [*lumières*] to give something satisfying in geography; for the relations that voyagers give us are not of sufficient help to confirm the topographical detail of the lands that they have traveled through. It would be necessary for these voyagers to be instructed in mathematics" (de Vaugondy 1757, quoted in Wolff, *Inventing Eastern Europe*, pp. 148–49).

Elsewhere, however, French cartographers were active in inscribing the new cartography of eastern Europe. The Cartographic Office established by Peter the Great was directed by Guillaume de L'Isle's brother. D'Anville was a corresponding member of the St. Petersburg Academy of Sciences. And the mapping of Poland, commissioned by Stanislaw August, was undertaken by the French surveyor Charles de Perthees (Wolff, *Inventing Eastern Europe*, pp. 146–47).

In the process, these mapmakers began to make visually evident the emerging distinction between "Europe" and "Les Estats du Sultan." No longer is the Ottoman world depicted as a single geographic unit as had invariably been the case in the folio atlases of Ortelius, Mercator-Hondius-Jansson, Blaeu, and other late sixteenth- and seventeenth-century cartographers. Sanson had been one of the first to break up the Ottoman empire into *Les Estats de l'Empire des Turqs en Asie* and *Estats de l'Empire des Tvrqs en Evrope*, but by the middle of the eighteenth century this division had been accepted by most European cartographers (figs. 20–21). Wolff argues that the paradox of "Turquie en Europe" — of Europe yet located outside Europe — was essential to the emerging idea of Europe during the Enlightenment and to the post-Karlowitz imperial ambitions of Austrian and Russian statesmen, irrespective of their military and political success in "repossessing" the lost lands of Europe. That mapping was central to these political ambitions, and to the geographical mastery and scientific penetration of Ottoman lands in Europe, is clearly conveyed in d'Anville's *L'Empire Turc* (1772), where he writes that the light of geography must "penetrate" Europe's remaining darkness so that the benefits of science can be brought to a region of uncultivated barbarism.

Quite how the practices that by the end of the eighteenth century had come to define European cartography found thier way into Ottoman mapping has not been closely studied. M. Pınar Emiralioğlu, in her essay in this volume, points to the rich and extensive tradition of Ottoman geographical mapmaking between the mid-fifteenth and

FIGURE 20. Nicolas Sanson. *Les Estats de l'Empire des Turqs en Asie.* Paris: Chez Pierre Mariette, 1652. The O. J. Sopranos Collection

mid-eighteenth centuries, which both contributed to and was informed by developments in European cartography. The writings of Katib Çelebi (A.H. 1017–1068 [A.D. 1608–1657]), and others like him, have often received particular attention, in part because of his translation of Mercator's *Atlas minor*, and in part because a version of his great geographical synthesis, *Cihan-nüma [View of the World]*, was among the earliest publications of the first Ottoman printing press (Faroqhi, *Ottoman Empire and the World*, p. 199). For European cartographers like d'Anville, the *Cihan-nüma* was valued for the systematic descriptions, collected from a variety of sources, of those parts of the Asian continent that were still unfamiliar to European travelers. Not unlike their European counterparts, Katib Çelebi and his contemporary, Ebu Bekir ibn Bishram el-Dimaşki, saw their work as both an intellectual and practical undertaking intended to enhance knowledge of the outside world among the Sultan's advisers and educated subjects.

However, Hagen rightly cautions against the tendency to measure Ottoman geographical accomplishments in terms of developments in western intellectual and scientific thought and argues that, while Katib Çelebi took from European knowledge, "in his way of thinking [he] remained thoroughly Ottoman" (Hagen, "Ottoman Geographical Writings," p. 185). He also points to a parallel, though little studied, tradition of Ottoman cosmographical writing and mapping comprising elements of astronomy and mathematics together with Islamic science, history, and classical literature that flourished alongside the more descriptive regional geography of Katib Çelebi well into the eigh-

FIGURE 21. Nicolas Sanson. *Estats de l'Empire des Turqs en Europe ....* From [*Atlas françois*]. Paris: Chez le Sr. Iaillot ..., 1700. Vault Oversize Ayer 135 .S19 1692 pl. [95]. Courtesy of The Newberry Library, Chicago

teenth century. He suggests that one reason for the continuance of this tradition was that the beautifully illuminated cosmographies were appreciated for their aesthetic appeal just as much as for their practical information and spiritual knowledge. Absent from eighteenth-century Ottoman geographical writing, however, is the preoccupation with what European mapmakers and map users increasingly promoted as a scientific model of collecting, measuring, and presenting geographic information. Against this background, the map of the western Mediterranean, taken from a world atlas published in Istanbul in 1803 (fig. 22), anticipates the gradual adoption of such ideas and practices in Ottoman cartography in the course of the nineteenth century. The atlas, *Cedid atlas tercümesi* [*Translation of the New Atlas*], was in fact prepared for use in the new Ottoman Military Engineering School. The maps in this atlas were taken from an edition of William Faden's *General Atlas* that had been acquired by Mahmud Ra'if Efendi while acting as private secretary to the Ottoman ambassador in London (see fig. 51). Translated into Ottoman Turkish and with all the maps re-engraved, the atlas was intended to introduce students and faculty in the new school to contemporary European cartographic practices, and as such was linked to late eighteenth- and early nineteenth-century efforts to transform and modernize the Ottoman military. Only fifty copies of the atlas were printed, including a presentation copy for Selim III, but from this point onwards Ottoman maps increasingly reflect European geographical science and cartographic practices (Karamustafa, *Military, Adminsitrative, and Scholarly Maps*, p. 218).

Figure 22. [William Faden]. [*The Western Mediterranean Sea*]. From *Cedid atlas tercümesi* [*Translation of the New Atlas*]. Üsküdar [Istanbul]: Tab'hane-yi Humayun'da, sene 1218 [1803]. Vault Baskes + G1019. T2 1803. Courtesy of The Newberry Library, Chicago (Gift of Roger S. Baskes)

ISMA'IL ABU AL-FIDA

Few visitors to the exhibit European Cartographers and the Ottoman World, 1500–1750: Maps from the Collection of O. J. Sopranos will recognize the name of the early fourteenth-century Arab geographer Abu al-Fida (A.H. 672–732 [A.D. 1273–1331]), yet his ideas and commentaries informed many of the maps and texts on display. His geography, *Taqwim al-buldan* [*The Study of Countries*] connects Gastaldi's map of Asia with Ramusio's great travel compendium, *Delle Navigationi et Viaggi*, and both with Ortelius' *Theatrum Orbis Terrarum*. The author of the text accompanying Hajji Ahmed's cordiform world map claims that it was Abu al-Fida's words on the importance of geographical knowledge to rulers and princes that provided the inspiration for the map, while Ramusio reproduces Abu al-Fida's geographical tables to assist cartographers in locating the cities visited and described by Marco Polo. That Abu al-Fida's work was of equal interest to Ottoman geographers and their patrons is clear from a late sixteenth-century abridgement of his text translated into Turkish by Muhammed bin Ali Sipahazade and presented to Sultan Murad III.[a]

The momentous change in European knowledge of the world that was set in motion during the Renaissance, and how that geographical knowledge was acquired, transmitted, and mapped, is an important part of the story of the exhibit. Abu al-Fida's observations and geographical texts tell us a great deal about the importance of classical sources in this undertaking and the flow of geographical information across cultural boundaries. They also speak to the cartographic accomplishments of Arab geographers in their own right, particularly their delineation and elaboration of the Greek mapping tradition and how Arab cosmographical knowledge found its way into European geographic thought and practice. Brought to the attention of European mapmakers in the mid-sixteenth century, Abu al-Fida's text was still cited as an authority by the French cartographer Jean Baptiste Bourgignon d'Anville in the late eighteenth century. That the continuing regard displayed by cartographers for Abu al-Fida's observations is accompanied by academic squabbling and imprisonment by the Inquisition adds color to the account of his work and its influence on later cartographic practice.

Abu al-Fida was a person of influence and pre-eminence in his own day, enjoying a reputation among his contemporaries as a patron of literature and science as well as a scholar in his own right. A member of the powerful Ayyubid dynasty, he entered the service of the Mamluk Sultans of Egypt after the suppression of the Ayyubid principality of Hamah in the late thirteenth century, and rose to a position of some importance in the provincial administration of Syria. He accompanied the Mamluk Sultan to Mecca in A.H. 719 (A.D. 1319/1320) and was rewarded for his service and loyalty by being publicly invested with the insignia of the sultan and granted precedence over other provincial governors in Syria (*Encyclopedia of Islam*, 1960).

Among Renaissance humanists, Abu al-Fida's geographical and intellectual reputation rested on two texts, both largely compilations of earlier works but re-arranged and supplemented by his own observations. The first was a universal history from the pre-Islamic period to his own times that, judging by the number of copies and extensions, appears to have been well regarded by his contemporaries. The second was the *Taqwim al-buldan* that seems to have been completed in A.H. 721 (A.D. 1321). This was primarily a descriptive geography compiled from a variety of sources, including lengthy passages from the twelfth-century Arab cosmographer and mapmaker al-Idrisi, but it followed the usual format of such geographies by including a series of tables listing place names with their geographical coordinates. It is difficult to assess Abu al-Fida's own contribution because for the most part the geographic data are taken from earlier Arab translations of Ptolemy, with divergences and differences noted. However, Abu al-Fida also includes additional information for places not listed by Ptolemy derived from the independent observations of other Arab geographers, notably al-Biruni.[b] Abu al-Fida's work appears to largely replace earlier geographical texts as a source of information for scholars during the later years of classical Islamic cosmography (*Encyclopedia of Islam*, 1960).

Knowledge of Abu al-Fida's work reached European humanist circles through the French oriental scholar and linguist Guillaume Postel, who acquired a copy of *Taqwim al-buldan* during a visit to the Levant in 1549–1550 (Kuntz, *Guillaume Postel*). Ramusio, in collecting geographical information for inclusion in his travel compendium, clearly had access to this text, which he describes as "Signore Ismael venuto diuinamente in luce à nostri tempi" ("divinely come to light in our times"), and the list of geographical coordinates for the places mentioned in Marco Polo's travel memoir taken from Abu al-Fida appears in the second volume of his *Delle Navigationi et Viaggi* published in 1559 (fig. 23). Quite how this information became available to Ramusio is unclear, but Postel lived in

Venice between 1547 and 1549, and was back in the city in 1553 after having again become *persona non grata* at the French court. During this later visit, Postel stayed at the home of the Giunti family, publisher of Ramusio's travel compendium, and it is hard to imagine that at some time during these visits Postel was not in contact with Ramusio, Gastaldi, and other members of the city's cosmographic circle debating the latest geographical theories and discoveries. Postel may even have had a role to play in introducing Fine's heart-shaped map of the world to the Venetian geographers (Mangani, "Abraham Ortelius," p. 68). However, Ramusio makes no acknowledgment of Postel's assistance, nor does Gastaldi identify the sources used in preparing his 1561 map of Asia, although there appears to be little doubt that he made use of Abu al-Fida's tables (Destombes, "Guillaume Postel cartographe," p. 362). Postel was clearly embittered by this experience and in a subsequent exchange of correspondence with Abraham Ortelius he complains that his work had been "stolen" by Gastaldi. Ortelius appears to have been sympathetic. In a note to the reader that appears on his 1567 map of Asia, he describes Gastaldi's earlier map as "*secundum traditionem Abilfed*[*a*]*e Ismaelis cosmographi Arabi*" and acknowledges Postel's role in bringing knowledge of Abu al-Fida's cosmography to Europe. In a letter to Ortelius dated April 9, 1567, Postel expresses his gratitude for restoring to him the praise that had been denied him by the Italians (Destombes, "Guillaume Postel cartographe").

However, a more generous explanation for the Italians' omission may be found in Postel's own precarious situation during the period in question. His unorthodox views on a universal theology and a universal state, combined with his dabbling in cabalism and occult mysticism, brought him into conflict with both religious and political authorities. To some of his inquisitors his great interest in Arabic and Hebrew texts was seen as tantamount to heresy (Kuntz, *Guillaume Postel*, pp. 34–35). Appearing before the Inquisition in Venice in 1554 to defend his views, Postel remained under close questioning until a verdict was handed down the following year that his work manifested impiety. He was judged to be demented and delirious, a decision that probably spared his life, but he remained imprisoned in Rome until 1559. It seems reasonable to conclude that, notwithstanding Postel's later complaints about having been denied the praise and credit due to him, the more prudent course of action for Ramusio or Gastaldi was to avoid any public association with Postel at a time when he had been declared mad and his work condemned by the Inquisition.[c]

For all the efforts of sixteenth- and seventeenth-century cartographers such as Gastaldi and Ortelius to provide more accurate geographical information, Jean de la Roque still writes despairingly at the beginning of the eighteenth century about the absence of a reliable map of the Arabian peninsula, noting that the only source of information "of use for a thorough understanding of the geography of Arabia" is Abu al-Fida (de la Roque, *Voyage to Arabia Felix*, p. xi). De la Roque's own translation of Abu al-Fida's description of Arabia appeared as an accompaniment to an edition of Laurent d'Arvieux's *Travels in Arabia Deserta*, first published in Paris in 1717. Continuing the line of authority begun with Ptolemy and reiterated by Ramusio, de la Roque compiles a table showing the latitude and longitude of towns in Arabia as provided by Abu al-Fida (fig. 24). De la Roque was the son of a French merchant who had traveled to Istanbul and Damascus, and, perhaps stimulated by his father's travels, de la Roque

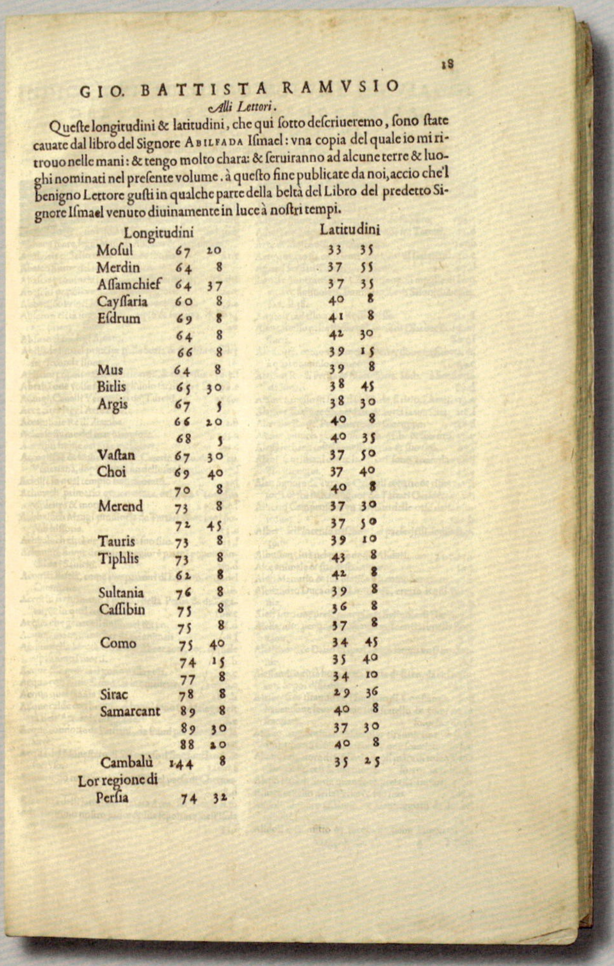

18

GIO. BATTISTA RAMVSIO

Alli Lettori.

Queſte longitudini & latitudini, che qui ſotto deſcriueremo, ſono ſtate cauate dal libro del Signore Abilfada Iſmael: vna copia del quale io mi ritrouo nelle mani: & tengo molto chara: & ſeruiranno ad alcune terre & luoghi nominati nel preſente volume. à queſto fine publicate da noi, accio che'l benigno Lettore guſti in qualche parte della beltà del Libro del predetto Signore Iſmael venuto diuinamente in luce à noſtri tempi.

	Longitudini		Latitudini	
Moſul	67	20	33	35
Merdin	64	8	37	55
Aſſamchief	64	37	37	35
Cayſſaria	60	8	40	8
Eſdrum	69	8	41	8
	64	8	42	30
	66	8	39	15
Mus	64	8	39	8
Bitlis	65	30	38	45
Argis	67	5	38	30
	66	20	40	8
	68	5	40	35
Vaſtan	67	30	37	50
Choi	69	40	37	40
	70	8	40	8
Merend	73	8	37	30
	72	45	37	50
Tauris	73	8	39	10
Tiphlis	73	8	43	8
	62	8	42	8
Sultania	76	8	39	8
Caſſibin	75	8	36	8
	75	8	37	8
Como	75	40	34	45
	74	15	35	40
	77	8	34	10
Sirac	78	8	29	36
Samarcant	89	8	40	8
	89	30	37	30
	88	20	40	8
Cambalù	144	8	35	25
Lor regione di Perſia	74	32		

FIGURE 23. [Giovanni Battista Ramusio]. Tables of Longitude and Latitude of places mentioned by Marco Polo as compiled by Ramusio from Abu al-Fida. From *Secundo Volume Delle Navigationi et Viaggi* .... Venetia [Venice]: Stamperia de Givnti [1574].
Courtesey of The University of Chicago Library, Special Collections Research Center

studied Arabic, visited the Levant, and developed a particular interest in the coffee trade with Arabia (Phillips, "Introduction," p. vii). This led to a book, *Voyage de l'Arabie heureuse* (1716) compiled from correspondence and meetings with those who had been involved in the first French trading expeditions to Mocha on the Red Sea coast of Arabia early in the eighteenth century in an attempt to secure direct access to coffee.[d] In an "advertisement" to the reader that accompanied the English translation (1726), de la Roque observes that "I could have wished to have annexed to this relation a good map of all Arabia Felix; but upon reflection I found it would be to no purpose to pretend to succeed in it. It would indeed have been easy to put together what we know of Arabia in general: but this would have been to have multiplied errors, instead of correcting them: for no body has travelled so far into the inland parts of this great country, as to be able to give an exact description of it" (de la Roque, *Voyage to Arabia Felix*, pp. ix–x). The best map for his purposes, de la Roque reports, is that by Guillaume de L'Isle (printed in 1715), which is based on the geographies of "Edrisi and Abufelda; so that till farther discoveries shall be made, we may not flatter ourselves with having a piece which must equally please, in respect of its novelty, and the care that has been taken to render it exact" (de la Roque, *Voyage to Arabia Felix*, pp. x–xi).[e]

This was a situation that only began to change in the aftermath of the Royal Danish Arabia Expedition (1761–1767) and the publication of its geographical reports and observations by Carsten Niebuhr, the sole survivor of that expedition, such that European cartographers could "flatter" themselves that their maps of Arabia were "exact." However, the larger point here is the continuing reliance on Abu al-Fida's text and calculations by mapmakers well into the eighteenth century.

Notes

[a] Hagen ("Ottoman Geographical Writings," p. 188) concludes that the mathematical and historical geography of Abu al-Fida was important in the work of seventeenth-century Ottoman geographers, notably Katib Çelebi and Ebu Bekir ibn Behram el-Dimaşki.

[b] Among early Islamic scholars, no one was more familiar with Indian cosmography and science than the great early eleventh-century mathematician and astronomer al-Biruni. Al-Biruni's work incorporates elements of this tradition of geographical inquiry along with Persian and Greek scientific sources and theories.

[c] Postel's copy of Abu al-Fida's geography has not survived. In debt and faced with the costs of defending himself before the Inquisition, Postel sold many of his books and collected manuscripts to the Elector Palatine Ottheinrich (Kuntz, *Guillaume Postel*, p. 120). Following his release from imprisonment in Rome, Postel returned to Paris where for a brief time he was permitted to lecture publicly on cosmography, but by 1564 he was again under investigation and confined to a monastery (ibid., p. 141).

[d] The 1708–1710 French expedition had been organized by merchants from the Breton port of St. Malo intent on purchasing coffee directly from Mocha, by-passing the Ottoman and Indian middlemen who controlled the trade. Although the expedition returned with coffee that was of poor quality and more expensive than that offered for sale by the Dutch, this did not deter the St. Malo merchants from investing in a second expedition (1711–1713). On that occasion several members of the French party traveled inland in response to a request from a local ruler for medical treatment (Phillips, "Introduction").

[e] The English editor of the 1732 re-printing of de la Roque's *Voyage to Arabia Felix* was so critical of de L'Isle's map that he omitted it from the volume as being of little value.

of ARABIA. 355

The Longitude and Latitude of the Cities of ARABIA, contain'd in Abulfeda's Tables, together with their Climate and Geographical Situation, according to the most approved Authors.

Names of Cities.	Degrees of Longit.		Degrees of Latit.		Ptolemy's Climates.	Provinces or Regions.
	deg.	m.	deg.	m.		
Mecca	57	30	21	20	At the Begin. of the 2. Clim.	Hegiaz or Thahamah.
Medina	67	30	24		At the middle of the 2. Clim.	Hegiaz or Nagd.
Ailah	56	40	28	50	3. Clim.	Upon the Borders of the Peninsula of Arabia.
Madyan	56	20	29		Beginning of the 3. Clim.	Near Syria.
Tayma	60	30	26		End of the 2. Clim.	Near the Desart of Syria.
Tabuc	58	50	26		3. Clim.	Near the Desart of Syria.
Hagr	60	30	28	30	3. Clim.	Near Hegiaz.
Tadmor	52		34		4. Clim.	Desart of Syria.
Yanbo	64		26		2. Clim.	Upon the Sea-Coast near Hegiaz.
Khaibar	67	30	24	20	2. Clim.	Hegiaz.
Maghian	64		16		1. Clim.	Upon the Sea-Coasts of Yemen.

We have omitted in this Table the different *Longitudes* and *Latitudes* given to the same City, in *Abulfeda's*

FIGURE 24. [Jean de la Roque]. Tables of longitude and latitude of cities in Arabia as compiled by Jean de la Roque from Abu al-Fida. From [Laurent d'Arvieux], *Voyage fait par ordre du Roy Louis XIV dans le Palestine … Par D. L. R. [de la Roque]* Paris: Chez André Gailleau, M.DCC.XVII [1717]. Courtesey of The University of Chicago Library, Special Collections Research Center

THE MEDITERRANEAN TRADITION OF CHARTING

A very different view of the world, one that has its roots in practical seafaring, is to be seen in the navigational charts of mariners. Here is a graphic record of the sailor's own first-hand experience of navigating the oceans and finding safe anchorage, a record of wayfaring that is very different from the more intellectual approach of the humanist scholars and cosmographers who sought to use the language of geometry to convey a synoptic view of their "new" world. As Cosgrove expresses it, "while the mariner scans the horizon and interrogates the compass, the [cosmographer's] vision rises conceptually over the surface, escaping the contingencies of location and moment in order to grasp a cosmic order and regularity" (*Apollo's Eye*, p. 104).

Navigational charts, usually referred to as portolan charts, were already in common use in the Mediterranean well before the "rediscovery" of Ptolemy's *Geographia* or the appearance of the first printed maps in the fifteenth century.[24] Trading across the Mediterranean world using the newly discovered compass, mariners from the late thirteenth century onward began to produce charts that were quite remarkable for the accuracy with which they mapped the coastlines and enclosed waters of the Mediterranean and Black seas. The mapping of, in particular, the North African coastline and the Gulf of Sirte in fifteenth-century portolan charts is far superior to anything found in Ptolemaic atlases and, indeed, was hardly improved upon at this scale until the eighteenth century (Campbell, "Portolan Charts"). Despite the differences between these two approaches to mapping, both emerged from and were shaped by the exchange of ideas and information among the trading cultures and economies of the Mediterranean world. Campbell sees these two strands, the contrasting products of classical cosmographical ideas and of practical seafaring, as being "at times distinct but often hopelessly intertwined" (*Earliest Printed Maps*, p. 1). And if in general it seems that surprisingly little of the geographical knowledge acquired as a result of the maritime experience of Mediterranean sailors found its way into the earliest printed maps, clearly there was cross-fertilization.[25]

The exhibit European Cartographers and the Ottoman World includes a small number of sea charts and atlases that can only begin to suggest the richness of a tradition that encompassed both technical achievement and artistic virtuosity. But the visually striking portolan chart of the Mediterranean and Black seas by Domenico Oliva, the beautifully executed Ottoman *Deniz atlası*, the bound collection of manuscript charts owned by Lord Howard of Effingham, the English Lord Admiral at the time of the Spanish Armada, and the artistry of the late seventeenth-century Dutch cartographer Romeijn de Hooghe provide a glimpse of the expanding view of the mariner in an age of seaborne reconnaissance and commerce.

The basic structure and conventions of the portolan are displayed in the beautifully drawn and richly illuminated chart by Domenico Oliva (fig. 25). Drawn on vellum and hand painted, its focus is the coastline, along with information needed by the navigator to chart a course and find a safe landfall. On the "neck" of the chart, a vignette of the crucifixion of Christ "protects" the mariner, but the chart otherwise lacks any clear orientation, since it was intended to be rotated as needed in the course of the voyage. Place names follow the shoreline in an orderly, unbroken sequence and are inscribed pointing inland in order not to interfere with practical information about hazardous shoals and safe anchorages often depicted in exaggerated form. The interconnecting network of rhumb lines emanating from compass roses further indicates the nautical function of the chart. The Oliva chart also illustrates many of the other conventions of portolans, including the use of color (as in the use of red to pick out the names of the more important ports and to illuminate the Red Sea), and the accompanying displays of banners and topographic views of the great Mediterranean trading cities (particularly elaborated in the case of Venice and Genoa). As Campbell ("Portolan Charts") has pointed out, it is precisely these shared stylistic conventions and features that make clear the common lineage of portolan charts.

Scholars have expended a huge amount of time and effort in debating the origins of the portolan chart and the extent to which information was shared among chart makers.[26] Some have sought to assert a Catalan origin. Others have given credit for the first charts to Genoa. Yet others have advanced Portuguese claims, while arguments have even been advanced for earlier formative influences dating back to the classical era. Such efforts frequently seem rather parochial, serving to separate the charts from the broader flows of information and goods within the

FIGURE 25. Domenico Oliva. [*Manuscript Portolan Chart of the Mediterranean and Black Seas*]. 1568. Manuscript map on vellum. Vault Oversize Ayer MS map 16. Courtesy of The Newberry Library, Chicago (Gift of Edward E. Ayer)

Mediterranean. In this regard, the surviving work of the Jewish chart maker, Judah Abenzara, provides a real-world illustration of the circumstances under which these charts were produced and the ways in which this knowledge disseminated through the Mediterranean world (fig. 26). Little is known about his early life. His work is clearly in the style of the Catalan-Majorcan school, yet the surviving examples of his charts were produced in Alexandria in 1497 and 1500, while a third map, now lost, was executed in Safed in 1505. Roth ("Abenzara's Map") has made a persuasive case that Abenzara most likely learned his craft in Majorca, as an apprentice in the great school of medieval Jewish cartography that flourished on the island in the fourteenth and fifteenth centuries, but that he left the island following the expulsion of Jews from Spain by Ferdinand and Isabella in 1492. Abenzara's use of the Italian language for the legends in his charts suggests to Roth that, along with many other exiles, the chart maker had found his way to Italy and later moved to Alexandria, where he continued to practice his craft.

Abenzara's chart gives practical expression to what Brotton describes as the "shared commercial and intellectual space" of the Mediterranean world in the fifteenth and sixteenth centuries, where "cultural influences combined to produce trading mechanisms and objects, such as charts and language, that were not unique to any one culture" (*Trading Territories*, p. 106). That the charts themselves were valuable trade items is clear from a late fourteenth-century account of charts being shipped from Barcelona for sale in different Mediterranean ports, on one occasion with instructions that they should be bartered in Alexandria for a consignment of pepper (Campbell, "Portolan Charts," p. 437). In a sense, perhaps, portolan charts were a graphic example of the lingua franca used by mariners and traders throughout the Mediterranean world, a hybrid language employing a mix of Italian, French, Spanish, Arabic, and, increasingly in the sixteenth century, Turkish words, that was of such functional use that it remained in use in the ports of the Mediterranean until the nineteenth century.[27]

FIGURE 26. Judah Abenzara. [*Manuscript Portolan Chart of the Mediterranean*]. 1500.
Courtesy of The Library of Hebrew Union College, Cincinnati, Ohio

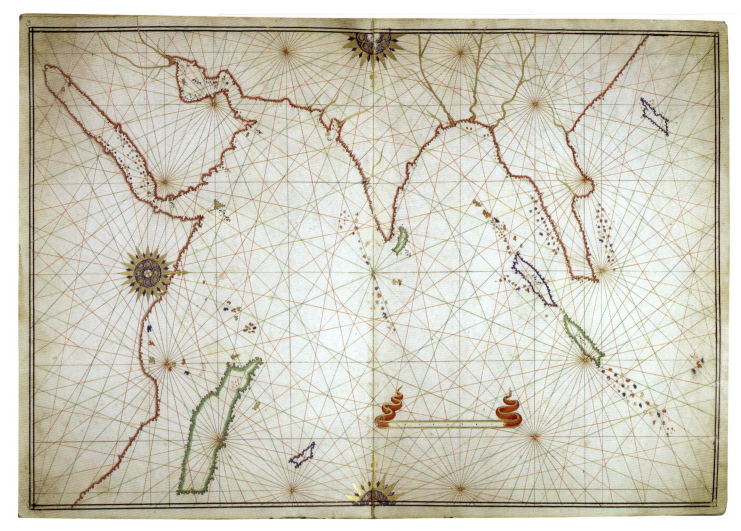

FIGURE 27. Chart of the Indian Ocean, from the *Walters Deniz atlası* [*Walters Sea Atlas*]. ca. 1560. Walters Art Museum W660, folios 7b–8a. Courtesy of The Walters Art Museum, Baltimore

The distinctive Ottoman contribution to this charting tradition is covered in the accompanying essay by M. Pınar Emiralioğlu, but if it is difficult to establish connections between portolan charts produced in the western Mediterranean and Ottoman activities associated with the making or use of sea charts, the handsomely illuminated *Walters Deniz atlası* [*Walters Sea Atlas*] leaves no doubt about the hybrid nature of the portolan tradition. The emergence of the Ottomans as the dominant naval power in the eastern Mediterranean closely followed the conquest of Syria and Egypt by Sultan Selim I in 1516/1517, but the Ottoman state had already begun to probe into the western Mediterranean as early as the 1480s, when Sultan Bayezid II had dispatched a naval squadron under Kemal Re'is to provide assistance to the Moors in Spain (Hess, "Evolution"). Indeed, it was during these early voyages to the western Mediterranean accompanying his uncle that Piri Re'is came to know many of the harbors and coasts of the region intimately, information that was later included in his *Kitab-ı Bahriye* [*Book of Maritime Matters*]. As Soucek notes ("Islamic Charting, pp. 262 ff.), the Tunisian chapters of the *Kitab-ı Bahriye* are particularly rich in detail and personal reminiscences that far exceed anything found in Italian or Catalan sailing directions and charts that have survived from this time.

Although portolan charts were shaped by and intended for practical use, two handsomely illuminated portolan atlases, both dating from the second half of the sixteenth century, one produced in Istanbul, the other prepared by Joan Martines for Lord Howard of Effingham, were clearly not intended to be taken to sea (figs. 27–28). Strikingly similar in style and geographic coverage, these atlases were produced for wealthy patrons and valued as much for their artistic and aesthetic qualities as for the geographic information they contained. Thus, alongside their practical role, chart making also existed within a system of client-patron relationships similar to that affecting the production of Ptolemaic maps and atlases.

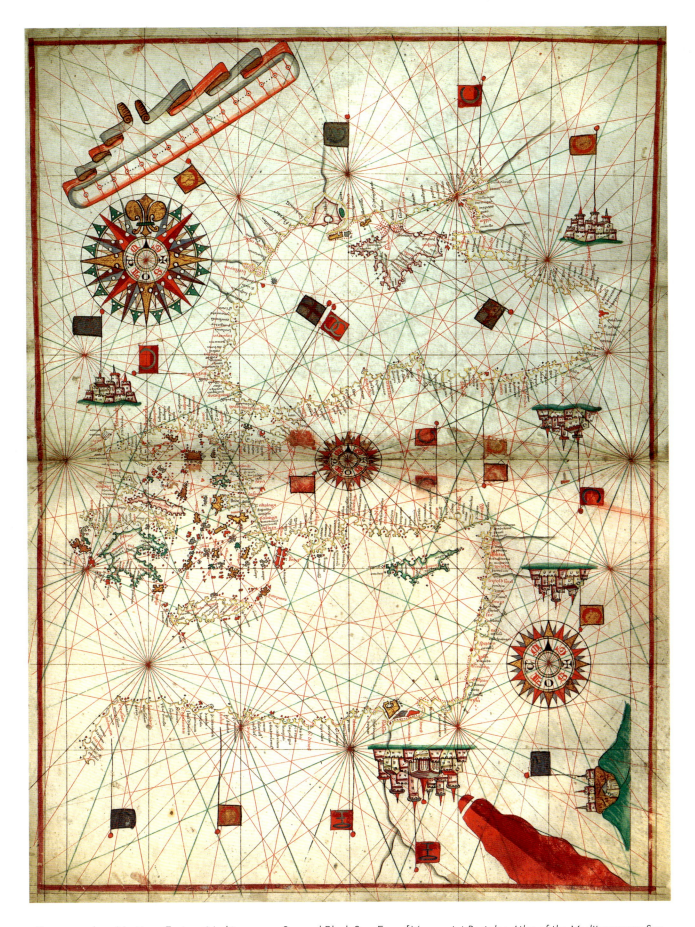

FIGURE 28. Joan Martines. Eastern Mediterranean Sea and Black Sea. From [*Manuscript Portolan Atlas of the Mediterranean Sea and the African Coast*]. 1583. Vault folio Ayer MS map 21. Courtesy of The Newberry Library, Chicago (Gift of Edward E. Ayer)

Later fifteenth- and early sixteenth-century portolan charts and atlases show coastlines well beyond the limits of the Mediterranean and Black seas and, indeed, often provide the first cartographic record of explorations across the Atlantic and into the Indian Ocean. By the end of the sixteenth century, however, it was the Dutch who had taken the lead in nautical cartography, and many of the Dutch cartographers who were publishing regional maps and world atlases were also engaged in producing the first printed sea charts and atlases.[28] The legacy from the portolan is clear in the style and formatting of the Dutch charts, but they also exhibited considerable innovation. Most notably, they now included hydrographic information derived from direct soundings and coastal surveying. Like the portolan tradition in the Mediterranean, Dutch navigators had access to pilot books containing sailing directions and to manuscript sea charts, but the publication of Lucas Janszoon Waghenaer's *Spieghel der Zeevaerdt* (literally "Mirror of Seafaring"), in 1584, was to sea charting what Ortelius' *Theatrum Orbis Terrarum* had been to regional mapping. Its charts of European coastal waters were the first to show depth soundings, to standardize the representation of hydrographic data, and to include views of the coastline in profile. "All these features combined to create a novel and practical working chart, indeed the measurement of depth against position in coastal waters came to be seen as the fundamental mark of the hydrographic chart" (Whitfield, *Charting of the Oceans*, pp. 67–69). The work proved immensely popular, and so dominant was the position of the Dutch in nautical mapping in this period that the word *waggoner* (after Waghenaer) came to be widely accepted in English (with variants in other European languages) as the term for a sea atlas.

Waghenaer's atlas included sea charts covering northern European coastal waters from the Baltic to the Straits of Gibralter, and it was Willem Barentsz' *Caertboeck van de Midlandtsche Zee* (1595) that extended the Dutch approach to nautical charting into the Mediterranean (Whitfield, *Charting of the Oceans*, p. 63). Barentsz was of course later to achieve greater fame as an explorer through his expeditions in search of the so-called Northeast Passage to east Asia. He was the first to sight Spitzbergen, but died in the course of a third expedition when his ships were trapped in the northern ice. Barentsz' map of the Mediterranean, *Thalassografica Tabula totius Maris Mediterranei*, is a fine example of Dutch nautical charting of the period, but also clearly reveals, in the alignment of place names, rhumb lines, and compass, the legacy of the portolan chart (fig. 29).

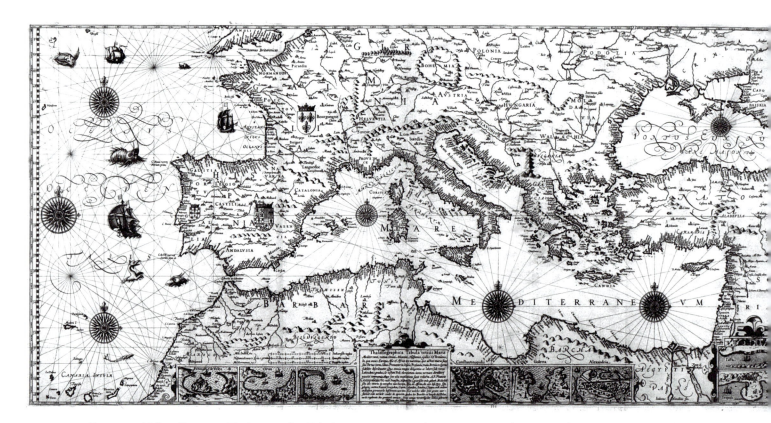

FIGURE 29. Willem Barentsz. *Thalassografica Tabula totius Maris Mediterranei.* Amsterdam, 1595. The O. J. Sopranos Collection

Carte Nouvelle
DE LA MER MEDITERANÉE
ou sont Exactement Remarquez tous les Ports, Golffes,
Rochers, Bancs de Sable &c A l'usage des Armées du Roy
DE LA GRANDE BRETAGNE, Dressée sur les Memoires
les Plus Nouveaux par le Sr ROMAIN DE HOOGE
A AMSTERDAM chez J. COVENS et C. MORTIER

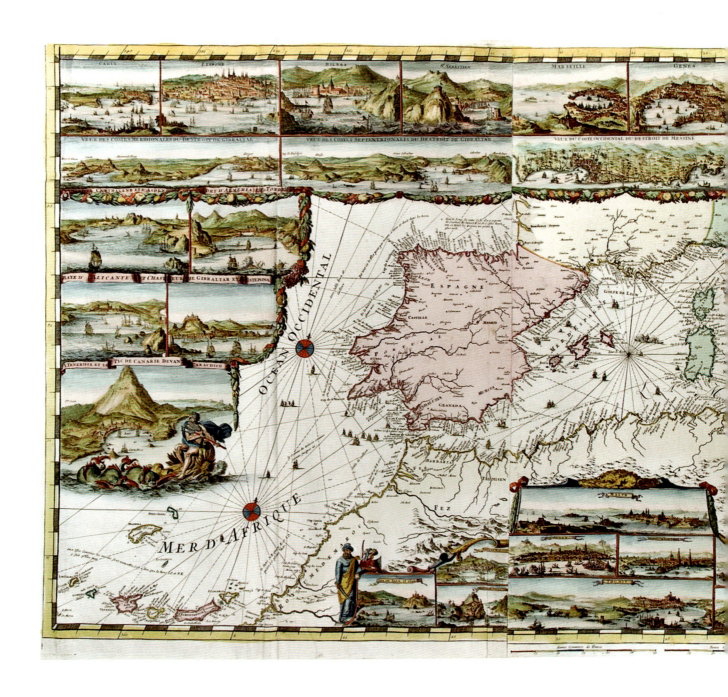

FIGURE 30. Romeijn de Hooghe. *Carte Nouvelle de la Mer Mediterranee où sont Exactement Remarqués tous les Ports, Golfes, Rochers, Bancs de Sable &c. a l'usage des Armées, du Roy de la Grande Bretagne.* 1711. From Pierre Mortier, *Atlas maritimus ....* Amsterdam: Chez J. Cóvens & C. Mortier. The O. J. Sopranos Collection

The inheritance from the earlier portolan tradition is equally clear in two seventeenth-century Mediterranean sea atlases on display in the exhibit. Hendrick Doncker's rare Italian-language chartbook, *Vera dichiaratione del Mare del Archipelago*, which covers the Aegean and eastern Mediterranean, is a reminder that this was first and foremost a practical undertaking. Published in Amsterdam in 1676, the charts were originally backed with an extra sheet of heavy paper for durability at sea. The charts in Francesco Maria Levanto's *Prima Parte dello Specchio del Mare*, published in Genoa in 1664, are also very much in the portolan style, complete with compass roses, rhumb lines, and alignment of place names along the coastline. In the Dutch style, Levanto adds lines of latitude and longitude and provides additional navigational aides including depth soundings on the charts as well as profile views of coastlines with landmarks observable from the sea. Levanto was a Genoese ship captain with many years experience of navigating in the Mediterranean. However, he worked from Dutch models and his atlas is a more or less direct copy of Pieter Goos' *Zee-Spiegel*, a striking affirmation of the prestige and dominant position enjoyed by Dutch chart makers during this period. In fact, Levanto's charts were widely copied and appropriated, and strongly influenced the development of maritime cartography in Italy (as evident in the work of Vincenzo Coronelli, who also produced a *Specchio*) over the next half century.

A final Dutch sea chart of the Mediterranean included in European Cartographers and the Ottoman World, Romeijn de Hooghe's magnificent *Carte Nouvelle de la Mer Mediterranee ...* illustrates how in the seventeenth century the sea chart was elaborated into what Whitfield (*Charting of the Oceans*) has characterized as "map art" (fig. 30). In such decorative sea charts and in the maritime paintings of such artists as the Van de Veldes, the Dutch "found a visual language in which to express their vital relationship to the sea" (ibid., p. 89). De Hooghe's chart was originally engraved for a maritime atlas published by Pieter Mortier in Amsterdam in 1694. In all, de Hooghe produced a series of nine charts for the atlas described by Koeman (*Atlantes Neerlandici*, vol. 4, p. 423) as "the most spectacular type of maritime cartography ever produced in seventeenth-century Amsterdam."

The Dutch dominance of the chart trade in the seventeenth century and the emergence of Amsterdam as the leading financial and trading center of northern Europe are clearly related events. The geographical knowledge that made these achievements possible is to be found, at least in part, in the travel narratives and maps of Jan Huygen van Linschoten (ca. 1563–1611), whose *Itinerario*, published in Amsterdam in 1596, included a remarkably accurate map of the Red Sea, Arabian peninsula, and eastern Indian Ocean (fig. 31).

Linschoten had spent six years in India as a personal secretary to the Archbishop of Goa, a Portuguese trading settlement on the western coast of India, but his family were Dutch Catholic merchants who had been able to continue doing business in Spain and Portugal despite the fact that Spain was officially at war with the Dutch United Provinces (Lach, *Asia*, p. 198). Linschoten seems to have made good use of his time in India. His *Itinerario* reveals a remarkable grasp of local and regional trade, politics, natural history, and social customs:

> From the Italian and English interlopers who arrived in Portuguese Goa, he learned about the land route. From Dutch sailors, gunners, and merchants in the service of the Portuguese, he gathered information about the places farther east. From his own experience on the return journey, when he was hired as a pepper factor ... he learned at first hand about the organization and structure of the spice trade under the contract system (Lach, *Asia*, p. 99).

Returning to Holland in 1592, at a pivotal moment in Dutch efforts to achieve political and commercial independence, Linschoten began working on his *Itinerario* but was encouraged by a circle of friends that included Lucas Janszoon Waghenaer and the map publisher Cornelis Claeszoon to put this work aside in favor of first publishing a description of the sea routes around Africa.[29] This was published under the title of *Reysgheschrift* [Mariner's Handbook]. What was most remarkable about Linschoten's handbook was the inclusion of many *roteiros*, or rutters (sea journals), compiled by Portuguese pilots in the course of eighty years navigating the Indian Ocean. Quite how or when Linschoten acquired these rutters is unclear, as they were zealously protected by the Portuguese, but they ensured that the information available to Dutch navigators and mapmakers was the latest and most accurate available. Moreover, by suggesting it was possible for the Dutch to steer directly for Java instead of the Malabar Coast of India, Linschoten pointed the way for successful Dutch entry into the East Indies trade. The value of his information is evident from the logbook of Cornelis de Houtman, the commander of the first Dutch expedition to the East

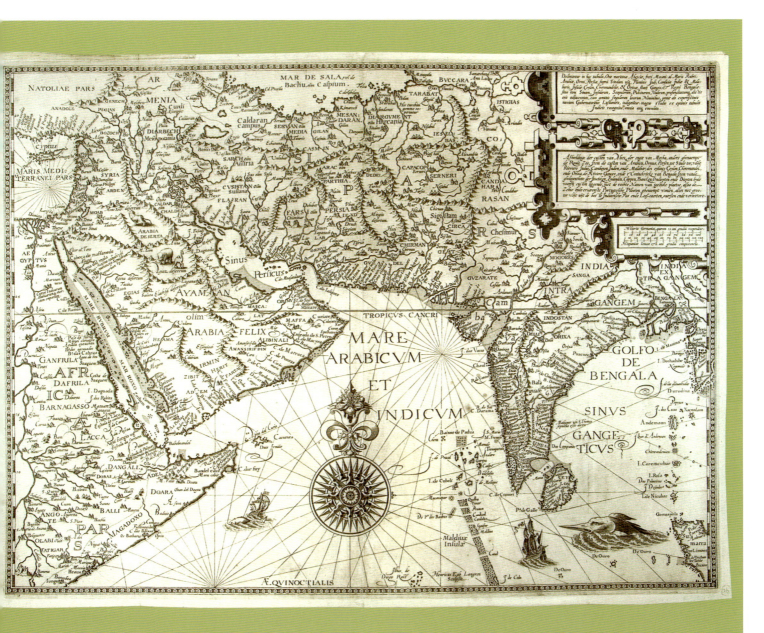

FIGURE 31. [Jan Huygen van Linschoten]. *Delineatuur in hac tabula, Oræ maritimæ Abexiæ, freti Meccani, al Maris Rubri, Arabiæ .... From Itinerario, Voyage ofte Schipvaert van Jan Huygen van Linschoten naar Oost-ofte Portugalis Indien.* Amsterdam: Cornelis Claesz, 1596.
The O. J. Sopranos Collection

Indies. It was the promise of this expedition that led to the formation of the Dutch East India Company, in 1602, and Houtman records that the *Reysgheschrift* had been given to him in manuscript form shortly before sailing (Parr, *Jan van Linschoten,* p. xvi). With information taken from the best Portuguese portolan charts of the Indian Ocean, the maps that were drawn by Henricus Langene for Linschoten's *Itinerario* were far more accurate than anything found in Gastaldi or Ortelius, and this information quickly found its way into the world and regional maps of Mercator-Hondius-Jansson and the Blaeus.

MAPPING THE CITY: *CIVITATES ORBIS TERRARUM*

A good prospect alone will ease melancholy .... What greater pleasure can
there be, than to view those elaborate maps of Ortelius, Mercator, Hondius, &c.?
To peruse those books of cities, put out by Braunus and Hogenbergius?

— Robert Burton, *The Anatomy of Melancholy.* 1621

One of the great geographical works of the sixteenth century was Georg Braun and Frans Hogenberg's monumental city atlas, *Civitates Orbis Terrarum*, published in six volumes between 1572 and 1617. As the name suggests, the work was inspired by Ortelius' *Theatrum Orbis Terrarum* (1570), and preparation of the two atlases must have overlapped. Hogenberg had engraved many of the plates for Ortelius' atlas, while Ortelius' support for the *Civitates* is clear from his correspondence with Braun. In the foreword to Book I of the *Civitates*, Braun generously acknowledges Ortelius as "the celebrated cosmographer of our day, [who] wonderfully enriched our work with the true descriptions of many cities" (Skelton, "Introduction," p. ix). Like the *Theatrum*, the *Civitates* was truly universal in its scope, and several views of cities within the Ottoman world appear in the work, including Istanbul (still identified as *Byzantivm nunc Constantinopolis*), Cairo (*Cairos, quae olim Babylon Aegypti maxima vrbs*), Damascus, and Alexandria (figs. 32–35).

FIGURE 32. Georg Braun and Frans Hogenberg. *Byzantivm nunc Constantinopolis.* [1572]. From *Civitates Orbis Terrarum*, Cologne. The O. J. Sopranos Collection

FIGURE 33. Georg Braun and Frans Hogenberg. *Cairos, quae olim Babylon Aegypti maxima vrbs.* [1575]. From *Civitates Orbis Terrarum*, Cologne. The O. J. Sopranos Collection

As Christine Boyer has observed, maps collapse both space and time, so that even the most remote places, once observed and fixed on a map, can be brought home and viewed right before one's eyes (Boyer, *City of Collective Memory*, pp. 206–09). In like manner, in promoting the *Civitates*, Braun writes of the pleasure of vicarious travel without the discomfort of traveling: "[w]hat could be more pleasant than, in one's own home far from all danger, to gaze in these books at the universal form of the earth ... adorned with the splendour of cities and fortresses and, by looking at the pictures and reading the texts accompanying them, to acquire knowledge which could scarcely be had but by long and difficult journeys?" (Braun and Hogenberg, *Civitates*, Book III). The success of this appeal can be judged by the number of translations and reprintings of the *Civitates* that appeared over the next one hundred years. So popular were Braun and Hogenberg's city views that the original plates were passed on through auction and inheritance until, sometime in the middle of the eighteenth century, they ended up in the hands of the Dutch publishers Johannes Cóvens and Corneille Mortier, who "used them until they were worn out" (Skelton, "Introduction," p. xxi). As the "defining" view of the cities they depicted, the images were often appropriated by other publishers who re-engraved them as illustrations for travel narratives and for use as "borders" to decorate and embellish regional maps and charts. This practice is illustrated in Romeijn de Hooghe's *Carte Nouvelle de la Mer Mediterranee*, where many of the views surrounding the map are taken from the *Civitates.*

FIGURE 34. Georg Braun and Frans Hogenberg. *Damascvs, vrbs noblissima ad Libanum montem, Totius Sÿria Metropolis.* [1575]. From *Civitates Orbis Terrarum*, Cologne. The O. J. Sopranos Collection

FIGURE 35. Georg Braun and Frans Hogenberg. *Alexandria, vetustissimum Ægÿpti emporium ....* [1575]. From *Civitates Orbis Terrarum*, Cologne. The O. J. Sopranos Collection

Just as city views emerged as a distinctive form of cartographic imagery in western Europe during the sixteenth century, there also developed a rich tradition of depicting the city in Ottoman painting and illustrated histories (Ebel, "City Views"). This finds its finest expression in the work of Matrakçı Nasuh, whose first-hand account of Sultan Süleyman I's campaign in eastern Anatolia, Persia, and Iraq during 1534/1535 provides a remarkable visual record of the imperial capital and the cities through which the army passed during the campaign (fig. 36). Matrakçı Nasuh's *Beyan-i menâzil-i sefer-i ʿIrâkeyen-i Sultan Süleyman Han* [*The Stages on Sultan Süleyman's Campaign in the Two Iraqs*], or, more succinctly, *Mecmuʾa-i menâzil* [*The Collected Stages*], was completed in ca. 1537 and represented an important development in Ottoman historical writing as a form of "official" record of actual events and imperial accomplishments. There had been earlier examples of Ottoman topographic mapping, notably military siege plans and the views of harbors and fortifications included in such maritime atlases as Piri Reʾis' *Kitab-ı Bahriye* (Karamustafa, "Maps and Plans"; Renda, "Representations of Towns"; Rogers, "Itineraries"). There was also a well-

FIGURE 36. Matrakçı Nasuh. [*View of Istanbul*]. From *Beyan-i menazil-i sefer-i 'Irakeyn-i Sultan Suleyman Han* [*The Stages on Sultan Süleyman's Campaign in the Two Iraqs*]. Ca. A.H. 944 (A.D. 1537/1538). TY. 5964. Courtesy of the Istanbul University Library

established practice of illustrating with topographic views the narratives of those who had undertaken the hajj to the Holy Cities of Mecca and Medina (fig. 37). But the use of city images as a way of conveying information about particular historical events, what Ebel has described as the narrative content of these images, is one of the more striking developments in sixteenth-century Ottoman cartography. In Matrakçi Nasuh's *Mecmu'a-i menâzil* these images form an itinerary, starting from Istanbul, the point of departure for the campaign, and progressing eastward in a manner that Ebel suggests is intended to convey the symbolic extension of imperial power and authority out to the remoter provincial cities of the empire. The fact that Matrakçi went on to produce two more volumes of contemporary Ottoman history that featured topographic views suggests that his approach to visualizing and mapping the geographical reach of the Ottoman empire was well received. Matrakçi's influence is clear in later illustrated

FIGURE 37. Ahmad Ardarumi. [*Views of Medina and Mecca*]. From *Kitab dala'il al-khairat wa shawariq al-anwar fi dkikh al-salat 'ala al-nabiyy al-mukhtar*. Copy of an original fifteenth-century manuscript (attributed to al-Jazuli al-Simali, 1465) by Ahmad Ardarumi (Ahmad of Erzurum?), dated to A.D. 1764/1765. OIM A12048. The Oriental Institute, University of Chicago

histories, where Ottoman artists and mapmakers become even more versatile and accomplished in weaving together pictorial images of historical events with the documentation of urban topographies (Ebel, "City Views").

In a similar fashion, early city views appearing in western Europe were often linked with specific historical events. The view of Tunis in Braun and Hogenberg's *Civitates Orbis Terrarum*, for example, narrates a series of actions during the attack on the city (at that time under the protection of the Ottoman admiral, Hayreddin Barbarossa) by Habsburg forces in 1535 as part of an effort to prevent Ottoman expansion into the western Mediterranean (fig. 38). However, while Ottoman city views continue to be explicitly linked to historical narratives, the development of topographic mapping elsewhere in Europe reflects the experimentation of Renaissance artists and mapmakers with mathematical rules of perspective as a way of achieving greater realism and accuracy. What was important in this tradition was to describe and portray the city such that "the reader seems to be seeing the actual town or place before his eyes" (Braun and Hogenberg, *Civitates*, Book III). By the mid-sixteenth century, engravings and woodcuts of cities were invariably being described as true and lifelike (*ad vivum*), and in advancing this proposition, Braun repeatedly emphasizes that the views in the *Civitates* are based, not on textual sources or written accounts, but on direct observation by the artist. Only in this way, through the sharpest sense of sight, could one hope to gain a true and accurate understanding of the city (Nuti, "Perspective Plan").

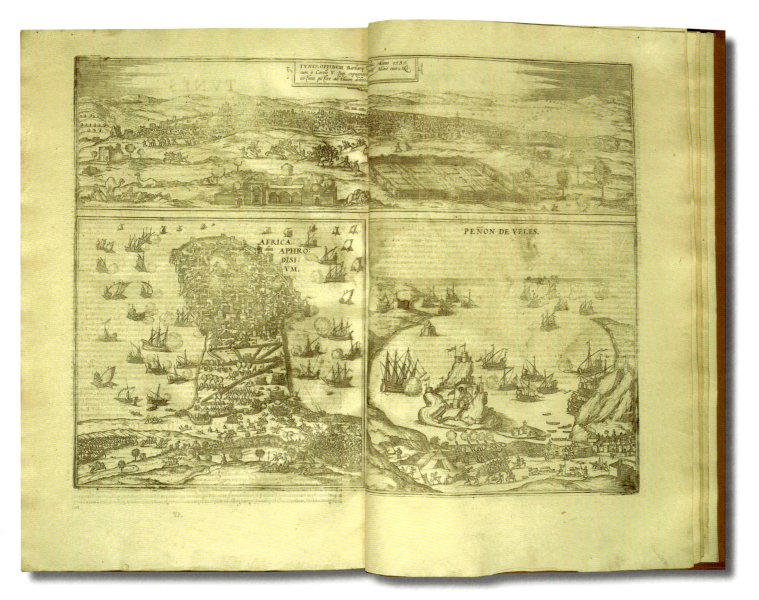

FIGURE 38. Georg Braun and Frans Hogenberg. *Tvnes, Oppidvm Barbarie ....* [1575]. From *Civitates Orbis Terrarum*, Book II. Cologne, 1633. Courtesy of The University of Chicago Library, Special Collections Research Center

FIGURE 39. *Hostantinopoli* [*Constantinople*]. From a manuscript copy of the *Geographia* prepared for the King of Naples ca. 1456. Paris BN Lat. 4802. Attributed to Pietro del Massaio. Courtesy of the Bibliothèque Nationale, Paris

Nuti ("Perspective Plan") makes a persuasive case that the development and refinement of the perspective plan, or bird's-eye view, during the fifteenth and sixteenth centuries was closely linked to these broader humanist concerns with "truthfulness." Hogenberg's engravings from the *Civitates*, beautifully composed to show the major landmarks and monuments of individual cities in considerable detail, are among the finest examples of this new "representational language." Such an approach to viewing and mapping the city was further justified by referring to Ptolemy's basic distinction between geography and chorography, the former being concerned with exactitude and representing the whole known world, the latter with the "smallest conceivable localities," where the intention should be to "paint a true likeness and not merely to give exact position and size" (Miller, *Mapping the City*, pp. 19–20).

What is particularly striking about the perspective plan is the elevated vantage point from which the observer can look down into the heart of the city. So frequently are these views reprinted in urban histories and guide books that it takes quite a conscious effort on our part to fully appreciate what a remarkable achievement they represent. As Schultz comments, "[we] who have had the experience of air travel and see aerial photographs every day in the press are able only with difficulty to realize what an imaginative feat … [such] views represented in an age without the gift of flight. They are ideal visions, reproducing something seen in the mind but invisible to the eye" ("View of Venice," p. 430). But the result is a powerful visual impression of the city's spatial structure and topography. Particularly prominent in Braun and Hogenberg's map *Byzantivm nunc Constantinopolis* (fig. 32), for example, are

FIGURE 40. Hartmann Schedel. *Constantinopolis.* From *Liber Chronicarum.*
Nuremberg: Anton Koberger, 1493. The O. J. Sopranos Collection

the gardens and buildings of Topkapı Palace ("Seraglio novo dove habita el gran Turcho" [New Palace where Lives the Grand Turk]), the curious spiral tower and fortifications of Yediküle [the Castle of the Seven Towers] that dominates the southwestern approach to the city ("Castel novo dove sat el tesoro del gran Turcho" [New Castle where Is Kept the Treasury of the Grand Turk]), the shipyards on the Golden Horn, and the imperial mosque of Sultan Mehmed II, all features of the massive rebuilding of the city begun by Mehmed following the Ottoman conquest of 1453 and continued by his successors.

For all their sophistication and lifelike appearance, it is important to note that the views are far from being an accurate historical record of these cities as they appeared in the second half of the sixteenth century. Most of the engravings were taken from whatever pre-existing models were available to Braun and Hogenberg. Thus the view of Istanbul is actually a re-engraving of a woodcut by Giovanni Andrea Vavassore that probably dates from the period 1535–1540, which, judging by its historic content, was itself derived from a late fifteenth-century drawing or sketch (Manners, "Constructing the Image"). Similarly, the engraving of Cairo (fig. 33) is taken from an earlier woodcut attributed to Matheo Pagano (ca. 1549). This too appears to have been composed a good deal earlier in the century, as such features as the aqueducts supplying water to the city are shown as they were located at the beginning of the sixteenth century (Codazzi, "Descrizione del Cairo"). As a result of the recycling of these views of Istanbul and Cairo, and subsequent reprintings of the *Civitates*, the same image, fixed in time, is perpetuated over a span of nearly three hundred years, a representation that, for all the claims of truthfulness, was far removed from the city as it actually appeared in 1572 when the city atlas first circulated, or even, for that matter, at the time of Vavassore and Pagano's woodcuts.

FIGURE 41. Untitled Map of Palestine. From Bernhard von Breydenbach, *Peregrinatio in Terram Sanctam*. Mainz: Erhard Reuwich, 1486. Courtesy of The Smithsonian Institute, Washington, D.C.

While the *Civitates* was a monumental achievement, it was not of course unprecedented in its interest in cities and topographical mapping. As Miller (*Mapping the City*) has noted, some of the earliest known collections of city views appear in manuscript copies of Ptolemy's *Geographia* produced in Florence in the mid-fifteenth century. These early attempts to apply the new science of perspective to topographic mapping are rather crudely executed, but they are distinctly different from the more generic views of cities in medieval histories and chronicles that make little attempt to show the city's actual topography and appearance with any degree of realism. Examples of this approach to composing and organizing the space of the city in its "true likeness" appear with increasing frequency in murals, frescoes, and narrative paintings during the fifteenth century, as well as in the well-known view of Constantinople that accompanies fifteenth-century manuscript copies of Buondelmonti's *Liber insularum archipelagi* (Manners, "Constructing the Image"). In fact, the view of Constantinople found in mid-fifteenth-century manuscript Ptolemy atlases (attributed to the artist Pietro del Massaio) is based on Buondelmonti's prototype, and like other versions offers a crude but recognizable view of the city and its surroundings with particular emphasis on those buildings, churches, and monuments that were seen as part of its Christian heritage (fig. 39). Thus Hogenberg's beautifully engraved plates for the *Civitates* are rooted in an artistic tradition that predates the appearance of printed topographic views and plans.

The earliest printed city views included in the exhibit are from Hartmann Schedel's *Liber Chronicarum*, printed in Nuremberg in 1493 and usually referred to as the *Nuremberg Chronicle* (fig. 40), and Bernhard von Breydenbach's *Peregrinatio in Terram Sanctam*, first published in Mainz in 1486 and which Campbell describes as the first illustrated travel book (*Earliest Printed Maps*, p. 93). Schedel's bird's-eye view of Constantinople, with the Byzantine double eagle still prominently displayed on the seawalls, repeats many of the details found in Buondelmonti's map. The church

of Hagia Sophia is prominently depicted, as are the harbor fortifications, the double line of walls and towers defending the land approaches to the city, and a number of monumental columns; Berger and Bardill ("Representation of Constantinople," p. 7) suggest that Buondelmonti was an important source of information for Schedel.

More impressive in terms of artistic and technical accomplishment are the remarkable woodcuts of places visited by Bernhard von Breydenbach, Canon of Mainz Cathedral, on his pilgrimage to Jerusalem in the years 1483–1484. These are the work of Erhard Reuwich of Utrecht, described by the author of *Peregrinatio in Terram Sanctam* as a "skilful painter" who went on the pilgrimage, and his woodcuts are filled with lively details that are clearly based on first-hand observation. Reuwich's map of Palestine, for example, is a striking topographic view (oriented with east at the top) extending from Sidon to Alexandria and from Damascus to Mecca (fig. 41). In its representation of local geography and general awareness of spatial relationships it is far superior to anything found in the Ptolemaic atlases of the period. Jerusalem, which dominates the central portion of the map, is shown from a birds'-eye perspective, and Reuwich faithfully represents most of the buildings and monuments of importance to pilgrims. Colorful details include the pilgrims disembarking from their galley in the port of Jaffa before setting off overland, while within the city the author identifies places where indulgences can be obtained with a note about their respective merits and costs (Davies, *Bernhard von Breydenbach*). The accurate rendition of the reconstructed twelfth-century facade of the Holy Sepulchre attests to the authenticity of the image and satisfied the Renaissance desire to see things "as if from life." Evidence of the appeal of these views comes from a contemporary, Brother Felix Fabri, who accompanied the Breydenbach group and later wrote his own account of the journey: "If anyone wishes to see the form of this church [of the Holy Sepulchre] let him look at the pilgrimage written by Lord Bernhard de Braitenbach ... where he will be able to see its own image drawn clearly as if he were standing in the courtyard and beholding it with his own eyes" (quoted in Miller, *Mapping the City*, p. 143).

Matthäus Merian's familiar engraving of Istanbul (fig. 42) falls very much within this tradition of pictorial mapping intended to convey a sense of place, and perspective and panoramic views of the city remained popular throughout the sixteenth and seventeenth centuries. However, Fr. Kauffer's *Plan de la Ville de Constantinople et de ses Faubourgs ...* (1776) marks something of a watershed in the mapping of Ottoman cities by European cartographers (fig. 43). The mathematical basis for the ground plan and the surveying instruments that made its construction possible had been perfected well before the end of the sixteenth century, but Kauffer's plan is one of the first attempts to apply these methods to a city in the Middle East. This more abstract record of the city's urban topography is very much in keeping with the scientific spirit of Enlightenment cartography, where the need for exactitude, whether driven by plans for urban improvement or the desire to record property boundaries, takes precedence over appearance. John Pinto ("Origins and Development") suggests that one reason for the relative scarcity of the iconographic plan until the mid-eighteenth century was the familiarity and versatility of bird's-eye views which better served the needs of armchair travelers, but from the mid-eighteenth century the city plan, with its carefully delineated streets and buildings shown in outline, becomes the only acceptable scientific measure of the city in western cartography. Perhaps it is possible to see a continuation of Ptolemy's chorographic tradition in the topographical paintings and views of nineteenth-century European landscape painters, but as Ronald Rees has commented, there is a certain irony in the fact that the achievements of fifteenth-century Renaissance artists in experimenting with perspective and envisioning the city in new ways initiated practices that two hundred years later encouraged surveyors and cartographers to dispense with their services completely (Rees, "Historical Links," p. 69).

16. Difes Oets ist angangen des Con- | 18. Stück von Constantini Pallast. | 20. Ein auffgemaurte garte von | 22. Arsenale. | 25. S. Iacobs Kirch | 28. Gefangnus thurn.
x stantini Pallast, biß zu ende Statt. | darin der T. K. Elephanten. | Cipressen beumen. | 23. S. Veneranda. | 26. Ein Hoche seule. | 29. Alte Seraglium, darin
17. Almazario. | 19. Constantini post. | 21. Ende der Statt, vnd Schlosses Constantini. | 24. S. Galatini kirch | 27. Ibrahim Bassan | das Frawenzimer.

FIGURE 42. Matthäus Merian. *Constantinopolis. Constantinopolitanæ vrbis effigies ad vivum expressa, qvam Tvrcæ stampoldam vocant.* From Johannes Angelius von Werdenhagen, *De Rebuspublicus Hanseatics.* Frankfurt: Merian, 1641. The O. J. Sopranos Collection

FIGURE 43. Fr. Kauffer. *Plan de la Ville de Constantinople et de ses Faubourgs tant en Europe qu'en Asie levé géometriquement en 1776.* From M. G. F. A. Comte de Choiseul-Gouffier, *Voyage pittoresque de la Grece.* Paris: J. J. Blaise, 1822. The O. J. Sopranos Collection

THROUGH THE EYES OF TRAVELERS

Un des plus grand avantages qu'un Voyageur pouvoit remporter de ses Voyages, etoit de se détromper des preventions qu'il a succees dans son Pais contre les Étrangers, don't ceux qui n'ent sont point sortis ne peuvent jaimais se défaire.

One of the greatest advantages that a Traveler is able to take back from his Voyages, is to be able to free himself from those prejudices that he has accepted in his own Country against Foreigners, from which those who are unable to leave will never be free.

— Laurent d'Arvieux, Chevalier, *Mémoires du Chevalier d'Arvieux*. 1673

The evolution of mapmaking between the sixteenth and eighteenth centuries cannot be separated from the flood of information about newly discovered worlds and faraway places brought back by travelers and voyagers. What preoccupied cartographers such as Giacomo Gastaldi, Abraham Ortelius, Gerardus Mercator, and Willem Blaeu was the preparation of maps based on the latest available geographic information. They borrowed freely (although not uncritically) from other cartographers and contemporary travel accounts in order to provide their readers and patrons with "maps [that] enable us to contemplate at home and right before our eyes things that are farthest away" (Joan Blaeu, quoted in Livingstone, *Geographical Tradition*, p. 98).

Although mapping is the primary focus of the exhibit European Geographers and the Ottoman World, a small selection from the extensive travel literature produced by visitors to the Ottoman world between the sixteenth and eighteenth centuries has also been included to illustrate the close connection between overseas travel and mapping.[30] As a number of authors have cautioned, it is difficult to document the influence of these materials, but they were clearly intended for a broad audience, while the frequency with which they were reprinted, translated, and copied suggests that they circulated widely and satisfied a growing demand for geographical literature. A reasonable inference is that it was essentially the written reports of travelers and the maps drawn from these accounts that provided the rest of Europe with its evolving geographic knowledge of the Ottoman world.[31]

Perhaps the most important feature of this travel literature is that it is so extensive and varied that it is impossible to categorize. Travelers came from different parts of Europe, for different purposes, and with very different interests and backgrounds. Nicolas de Nicolay, for example, was a military engineer whose maps and services to the French crown earned him the title *géographe ordinaire du roy*. He accompanied the French ambassador on a diplomatic mission to Istanbul in 1551, and his account of that visit has attracted considerable interest, in part because of the plates, made from Nicolay's drawings, of the local costumes and dress of different peoples and officials encountered during the voyage (figs. 44–45). Indeed, sixteenth- and seventeenth-century cartographers made frequent

FIGURE 44. Nicolas de Nicolay. *Giannizzerra andando alla Guerra [Ottoman Janissary Soldier]*. From *Le Navigationi et Viaggi, fatti nella Turchia ....* Venice: Francesco Ziletti, 1580. The O. J. Sopranos Collection

FIGURE 45. Nicolas de Nicolay. *Gentildonna Turca stando in casa sua ouero nel Serraglio* [Turkish Gentlewoman of the Seraglio]. From *Le Navigationi et Viaggi, fatti nella Turchia* .... Venice: Francesco Ziletti, 1580. The O. J. Sopranos Collection

borrowings of Nicolay's drawings for the borders of their own maps as a way of visually elaborating on the geography of the Ottoman empire. Mansell ("French Renaissance," pp. 101–02) questions the accuracy of Nicolay's rendition of these costumes and notes his clichéd view of Ottoman society and reliance on previously published books for much of his information. But Nicolay's skill as an observer seems to have been employed primarily as a spy, in collecting military information, sketching major fortifications, assessing the strength of garrisons and the number and size of canons – information that presumably was reported back to the French government (Karrow, *Mapmakers,* pp. 435-43). Nicolay writes of making "maps and geographical descriptions, topographic and chorographic, of the lands, cities, estates, and seas, with a very curious relief model of the city of Constantinople" (quoted in ibid., p. 437). These materials appear never to have been published and may well have been lost in the course of a disastrous fire in the eighteenth century that consumed Nicolay's extensive collection of maps and sketches.

Others traveled with very different motives and outcomes. Guillaume Postel, as described in the essay on Abu al-Fida, was interested in acquiring classical and Arabic texts, while Thomas Dallam, an accomplished musician and manufacturer of organ pipes, traveled to Istanbul in 1599 to deliver and demonstrate a clockwork musical organ, a gift from Elizabeth I to the new sultan, Mehmed III (MacLean, *Rise of Oriental Travel*). Oghier Ghiselin de Busbecq served as a Habsburg ambassador to the Ottoman Porte between 1555 and 1562 and was favorably impressed by the civil and military administration of the Ottoman empire. His letters, originally written to a fellow diplomat and published as a collected volume in 1589, provide a lively and informative account of Ottoman society and institutions, but Busbecq was also a keen naturalist. In his correspondence he writes about the menagerie of birds and animals he

has collected, including an infatuated crane, and, by bringing back a tulip bulb for a friend at the Royal Medicinal College in Vienna (along with a wagonload of manuscripts, coins, and other curios), is usually credited with introducing knowledge of tulip cultivation to northern Europe.

There was of course nothing new about such journeys by Europeans, the most notable being those of the Polo family in the thirteenth century, while religious pilgrimages to the Holy Land drew considerable numbers despite the hazards and risks involved. Moreover, as Deborah Howard points out, travel was an integral part of trade and diplomacy in Venetian culture, producing a considerable body of knowledge about the world beyond the eastern Mediterranean (Howard, "Status of the Oriental Traveller"). By the sixteenth century there existed sizeable resident Venetian colonies in places like Alexandria, Damascus, and Aleppo – places "that were so familiar that few Venetian visitors felt the need to describe them" (ibid., p. 30).

There were also precedents for providing a written account of such travels, as exemplified in Christopher Buondelmonti's *Liber insularum archipelagi* and Bernhard von Breydenbach's *Peregrinatio in Terram Sanctam.* Buondelmonti is known to have traveled widely in the Aegean in the early fifteenth century, visiting Constantinople on at least two occasions (Manners, "Constructing the Image"). By some accounts he was there to acquire classical manuscripts, but what distinguishes his narrative from those of earlier medieval travelers is the use of maps, *figurata*, to help readers visualize the islands he had visited and knew through first-hand observation (fig. 46). The *Liber insularum archipelagi* was most likely completed around 1418, and evidence that it appealed to a wide audience, at least by the standards of the times, is suggested by the number of manuscript copies that survive from the fifteenth and sixteenth centuries (Turner, "Christopher Buondelmonti," p. 13). In a preface to a version of the manuscript dedicated to Buondelmonti's patron, Cardinal Jordano Orsini, the author seems to anticipate the intentions of many later travel writers: "I have wished to send it to you … so that when you are tired, you can, with this book, bring pleasure to your mind" (quoted in Miller, *Mapping the City*, p. 111).

FIGURE 46. Christopher Buondelmonti. *Insula Crete.* From *Christoph. Buondelmontii, Florentini, Librum insularum archipelagi ….* Lipsiae et Berolini: Apud G. Reimer, 1824. Courtesy of The University of Chicago Library, Special Collections Research Center

Like Buondelmonti's *Liber Insularum*, Breydenbach's account of his pilgrimage to the Holy Land provides a striking visual record of the places that he and his fellow pilgrims visited en route. As described in more detail in the chapter *Mapping the City*, the woodcuts produced by the "skilful painter" Erhard Reuwich who accompanied the pilgrims are remarkable for their lifelike quality and depictions of local and regional topography. The woodcut of Rhodes (fig. 47), for example, is distinguished by the vivid portrayal of windmills, shipbuilding activities, the arrival of the travelers' galley with banners flying, and, as evidence of its detailed and careful observation, the damage inflicted on the harbor during the Ottoman siege of 1480 is clearly depicted (Davies, *Bernhard von Breydenbach*). Both Buondelmonti and Reuwich were important sources for later mapmakers, who borrowed freely and usually without attribution. Thus Buondelmonti's view of Constantinople was the source for Pietro del Massaio's map of that city appearing in later fifteenth-century manuscript copies of Ptolemy's *Geographia*, while his influence on later printed island atlases (*isolario*) is traceable in the work of Bartolemmeo dalli Sonetti, Benedetto Bordone, Tomasso Porcacchi, and others. Likewise, Reuwich's woodcut views were appropriated and embellished by many later authors for their own travel narratives, and by cartographers and editors such as Sebastian Münster (in his *Cosmographie*) and Georg Braun and Frans Hogenberg (for their *Civitates Orbis Terrarum*).

FIGURE 47. [Erhard Reuwich]. *Rhodis*. From Bernhard von Breydenbach, *Peregrinatio in Terram Sanctam*. Mainz: Erhard Reuwich, 1486. The O. J. Sopranos Collection

One of the important developments in the genre of travel literature in the sixteenth century was the effort by scholars to systematically collect earlier travel accounts (including many that had not appeared in print). The printing of travel compendia and geographies with critical commentaries comparing contemporary descriptions with classical sources became a major undertaking. The earliest and most influential of these great travel compendia was Giovanni Battista Ramusio's three-volume *Delle Navigationi et Viaggi*, published in Venice between 1550 and 1559. Ramusio's friendship with the foremost Venetian cartographer of the mid-sixteenth century, Giacomo Gastaldi, and the ways in which their collaboration produced a "new map" of Asia, has been covered in the introductory essay. Howard ("Status of the Oriental Traveller," p. 31) quotes a mid-sixteenth-century Venetian publisher, Antonio Manutio, as praising the efforts of merchants in collecting knowledge about distant lands, while noting that the problem was how to relate these new place names, which he called *nomi barbari*, to classical sources. Ramusio's intention was to address this need, and in the process he produced a source that served as a reference work for cartographers for the rest of the century.

While Ramusio's collection was explicitly intended to benefit cartography, it also served as a model for later compilations, notably those by two British editors, Richard Eden and Richard Hakluyt, as well as numerous more

popular anthologies that lacked Ramusio's scholarly approach. That Ramusio's work continued to be seen as meeting the highest scholarly standards is evident in the comment of the seventeenth-century English philosopher John Locke, who observed that Ramusio's geography was free from that "great mass of useless matter which swells our English Hakluyt and Purchas, much more complete and full than the Latin De Bry, and in fine is the noblest work of nature" (quoted in Lach, *Asia*, p. 208).

The printed anthologies of travel narratives brought these accounts before a much wider audience, contributing significantly to the shaping of geographical knowledge about faraway places. Moreover, as Howard has noted ("Status of the Oriental Traveller," p. 30), the very act of printing gave these accounts, often published in handsome formats and profusely illustrated with maps and views, a greater sense of authority and authenticity, while at the same time further stimulating interest in the possibilities of travel and trade. Alongside the anthologies and independent travel accounts, publishing houses produced a wide array of travel-related literature, including printed handbooks for merchants, travel guides, illustrated itineraries, and route maps. Gioseppe Rosaccio was a publisher who met this wider popular demand for cosmographies, illustrated world maps, and travel guides, and his *Viaggi da Venetia a Costantinopoli per Marre et per Terra …*, published in Venice in 1610, brings together many of the features of this genre of travel cartography. It is a compilation of previously published regional maps as well as maps of the Greek islands (somewhat in the tradition of the *isolario*) and views of towns and ports that follow the standard itinerary for those traveling between Venice and Istanbul in the first half of the seventeenth century. An exceptionally fine example of an illustrated itinerary, although one dating from the late seventeenth century and based on the traveler's own paintings and sketches, is Cornelis de Bruijn's *Reizen van Cornelis de Bruyn, door de Vermaardtse Deelen van Klein Asie …*, first published in 1698 but widely reprinted and translated. De Bruijn was first and foremost an artist who made two lengthy trips to the region, first to Turkey and the Levant and later to Persia. His profusely illustrated account of his travels suggests a particular interest in classical monuments, tombs, and religious sites, although among the most striking images are the remarkable fold-out panoramic views of cities (fig. 48).

A second important development affecting geographical writing on the Ottoman world during the sixteenth century was the growing number of travelers from northern Europe. As Murphey ("Bigots or Informed Observers?" p. 297) has observed, "beginning in the mid-sixteenth century … the broadening of both commercial and diplomatic contact [between the Ottoman state and the rest of Europe] stimulated a rapid proliferation of motives for

FIGURE 48. Cornelis de Bruijn. *Constantinopolis.* From *Reizen van Cornelis de Bruyn, door de Vermaardtse Deelen van Klein Asie ….* Delft: Henrik van Krooneveld, 1698. The O. J. Sopranos Collection

travel and types of travellers." He calls attention particularly to the French-Ottoman alliance against the Habsburgs beginning in the 1530s and the developing Anglo-Ottoman commercial ties during the late sixteenth century as exemplifying the wider context within which travel and cultural contacts evolved. It became customary for northern European powers to appoint permanent resident ambassadors at the Ottoman Porte, while the presence of growing merchant communities from northern Europe "encouraged the growth of multi-dimensional relations with various European states and revolutionized diplomatic practices .... Many of the traveler/observers of the seventeenth century came from this new breed of diplomat, and their accounts reflect a close familiarity with Ottoman affairs gained from long service and residence" (ibid., p. 297).

The French were especially prominent, and Mansell ("French Renaissance," p. 96) describes the French embassy in Istanbul from the arrival, in 1535, of the first ambassador, Jean de la Foret, as functioning as "Europe's window on the Islamic world." Far more books were printed in France in the sixteenth century on the Ottoman empire than on the Americas, while the Ottoman world continued to be the primary focus of French travel writing throughout the seventeenth century, as exemplified in the narratives of Jean-Baptiste Tavernier and Jean de Thévenot. Tavernier's *Les six voyages de Tavernier en Turquie, en Perse, et aux Indes*, first published in Paris in 1689, eventually appeared in a total of twenty-one French editions and was translated into English, Dutch, Italian, and German. His account of the six journeys he made to Turkey, Persia, and India between 1631 and 1668 is of particular interest in the context of mapping the Ottoman world, as he was one of the few travelers who had some training as a cartographer. His father, Melchior Tavernier, was the leading French publisher of atlases and sheet maps in the first half of the seventeenth century and his brothers were similarly engaged in the map publishing business. One of the striking features of Tavernier's account is his focus on the major travel routes through the Ottoman empire, with detailed discussion of distances and travel times, local trade and customs, and "holts" at each resting place, that are in some ways a textual version of the itinerary and route maps of French roads published by his father. But he was a good observer, and his narrative is illustrated with what he called "word paintings," views of towns, details of local architecture, sketches of flora and fauna, and maps of the region.

Like Tavernier, Jean de Thévenot was also considered by his contemporaries to be a reliable observer, and his journals were still being cited as a source by the French cartographer d'Anville late in the eighteenth century. Sundeen ("Thévenot the Tourist," pp. 6–7) draws attention to the way in which travelers like Thévenot prepared for

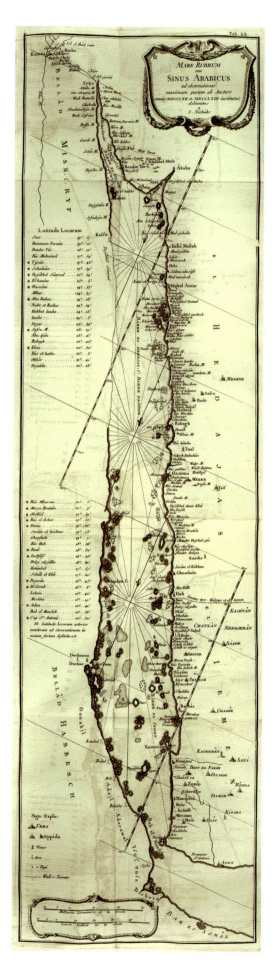

their journeys, consulting with scholars, making some attempt at least to master the language; moreover, Thévenot, in contrast to many of his contemporaries, attempted to talk to people from all walks of life and writes that he has sought to verify everything he reports from multiple sources. Here, perhaps, is an aspect of sixteenth- and seventeenth-century travel literature on the Ottoman empire that has not always been appreciated until recently. As Murphey has noted, what interested the travelers during this period were the practical details of Ottoman institutions, administration, trade, and society, rather than more sensational accounts of Ottoman lifestyles or descriptions of classical ruins and antiquities:

They were still prevented both by ignorance and prejudice from delving too deeply, but their eagerness to educate themselves is remarkable .... To their own interests and those of their readers anti-Muslim polemic was mostly irrelevant. What whetted their collective appetites most was news of the political situation, economic trends, market conditions, and the state of civil society (Murphey, "Bigots or Informed Observers?" pp. 299–300).

That is not, of course, to be naïve about the motives of travelers who were guided as much by self-interest as intellectual curiosity: Tavernier, for example, saw himself as a merchant-ambassador and his account of local markets, exchange rates, social customs, and commercial practices is framed in terms of "sage advice" necessary for a successful trade mission. Tavernier was particularly interested in locating the source of diamonds and other precious gems.[32] His notebooks are filled with drawings of various stones and methods of gem-cutting he had observed in Persia and India, and he made a fortune several times over in serving both Louis XIV and the French East India Company (founded in 1664) through the contacts and relationships he had forged with local rulers (York, "Travels in India"). Similarly, Jean de la Roque, whose critique of existing maps of Arabia in *Voyage de l'Arabie heureuse* has been noted in the essay on Abu al-Fida, was motivated by his interest in the efforts of French merchants from the Breton port of St. Malo to enter the coffee trade directly, bypassing the Ottoman and Indian middlemen who controlled the trade.

The broadening of diplomatic and commercial contacts between the Ottoman empire and the rest of Europe opened the way to travelers with a wider range of interests, particularly the growth of what might be termed "scientific travel." During the seventeenth century, botanists and naturalists in particular became identifiable new types of traveler who addressed separate readers with specialized interests (Murphey, "Bigots or Informed Observers?"). To a certain extent, the new scientific interest in such subjects as botany and medicine had been anticipated by earlier travelers like Rauwolf, Tavernier, and Thévenot. Leonhard Rauwolf is usually remembered as being the first European to describe the preparation and drinking of coffee: "a very good drink they call *Chaube* that is almost as black

FIGURE 49. Carsten Niebuhr. *Mare Rubrum seu Sinus Arabicus ....* From *Description de l'Arabie d'après les observations et recherches faites dans le pays meme. Par M. Niebuhr, Capitaine d'Ingenieurs, Membre de la Société Royale de Gottingen.* Paris: Chez Brunet, M.DCC.LXXI. [1779]. Courtesy of The University of Chicago Library, Special Collections Research Center

Figure 50. Carsten Niebuhr. *Terræ Yemen ....* From *Description de l'Arabie, d'Aprés les Observations et Recherches Faites dans le Pays Meme. Par M. Niebuhr, Capitaine d'Ingenieurs ....* A Copenhagen: Chez Nicolas Müller, MDCCLXXIII [1773]. Courtesy of The University of Chicago Library, Special Collections Research Center

as ink and very good in illness, chiefly those of the stomach" (quoted in Dannenfeldt, *Leonhard Rauwolf*, p. 71). But he was a physician and his three-year journey to the Levant, Anatolia, and Armenia between 1573 and 1576 was undertaken in part to identify and collect medicinal plants that might be profitably brought back to Germany (ibid.). Thévenot also was an avid naturalist and prepared an unpublished five-volume *Hortus Siccus*, listing and describing all the plants he had found on his travels (Sundeen, "Thévenot the Tourist"). But as Livingstone has noted (*Geographical Tradition*, pp. 125–26), the naturalist travel of the eighteenth century was characterized by a much more self-conscious determination to collect and catalogue materials as a scientific undertaking, an enterprise that was further stimulated by the establishment of plant repositories such as London's Kew Gardens and patronized by new scientific societies such as the British Royal Society and the French Académie des Sciences. "Throughout, a passion for precision characterized the whole enterprise: mathematical precision in astronomical observation, in cartographic accuracy, and in scientific illustration" (Livingstone, *Geographical Tradition*, p. 126).

Exemplifying the new type of scientific exploration was the Royal Danish Expedition to Arabia, undertaken between 1761 and 1767, of whom Carsten Niebuhr was the sole survivor. Initiated by the German Orientalist Johann Michaelis, who secured the patronage of King Friedrich V of Denmark, the expedition in many respects anticipates by nearly three decades the sort of exhaustive, all-encompassing, all-seeing approach to documenting local culture and geography that characterized the work of the naturalists, scientists, philologists, and archaeologists who accompanied Napoleon's expedition to Egypt. The original members of the Royal Danish Expedition included Niebuhr, whose role as surveyor and mathematician was to conduct astronomical and geographical observations; Frederick Christian von Haven, responsible for philological studies; Peter Forsskål for natural sciences; Christian Carl Kramer, who was to research medicinal plants and practices; and Georg Baurenfeind, a copperplate engraver to prepare sketches and graphic documentation. Nearly two years were spent preparing for the expedition; scientists from all over Europe were invited to submit questions, while detailed guidelines were developed as to how the expedition was to proceed with its investigations, record observations, and conduct relationships with local peoples. By 1764, after two years in Egypt, the Sinai, and Yemen, the surviving members of the expedition sailed from Mocha for India; within two months only Niebuhr remained alive. But the contribution of the expedition, particularly with respect to European geographical knowledge of Yemen and interior Arabia, was substantial. Niebuhr returned to Denmark in 1767 with a huge collection of specimens, sketches, manuscripts, and field notebooks filled with observations. Niebuhr's maps of Yemen and interior Arabia were to remain the standard source for cartographers until well into the twentieth century (figs. 49–50). In the notes accompanying his new map of Arabia, published in 1775 (fig. 51), the French cartographer Jean Baptiste d'Anville comments that, as a result of Niebuhr's precise observations, European cartographers now had access to reliable information on the region for the first time. In this vein, the Royal Danish Expedition to Arabia has sometimes been referred to as the "first modern research expedition" and certainly it was part of the opening up of the world to Enlightenment ideas and science that occurred during the eighteenth century. However, as Livingstone (*Geographical Tradition*, p. 125) cautions, "it would be mistaken to take the traveling naturalists' apologetic rhetoric of 'science for science's sake' at face value, for geographical knowledge was geopolitical power."

As the above brief account should make clear, the handful of travel accounts of the Ottoman empire from the early sixteenth century had become a flood by the end of the eighteenth century. Not surprisingly, there is no single overarching view of the Ottoman world that emerges from this literature; nor should this be surprising given the variety of circumstances, purposes, interests, and national backgrounds that shaped the travelers' perspectives, experiences, and appreciation for the places they visited. Certainly, there continued to be a popular literature that focused on what their authors saw as the strange and unusual customs and beliefs of the Ottomans. But it is also clear that much of the travel literature of the seventeenth and eighteenth centuries was considerably more thoughtful, practical, and perceptive than that of preceding centuries, or, for that matter, the more romanticized writings of the nineteenth century. As Murphey ("Bigots or Informed Observers?" p. 302) comments about travel accounts of the Middle East from this period: "what most distinguished the brief period of realistic writing about the Middle East during the seventeenth and eighteenth centuries ... was its credibility .... The pre-colonial orientalist-travellers often fell short of being 'perfect' observers, and their character and intellection was from irreproachable, but their accounts make lively and informative reading." And in general, travelers such as Oghier Ghiselin de Busbecq, Jean de

Figure 51. Jean Baptiste d'Anville. A New Map of Arabia Divided into Its Several Regions and Districts. [1775]. From William Faden, [*General Atlas: A Collection of Large-Scale Maps and Charts of All Parts of the World by Various Cartographers and Publishers*]. London: Laurie & Whittle, 1794–1816. Ayer 135 G32 1775, v. 2. Courtesy of The Newberry Library, Chicago

Thévenot, and Jean-Baptiste Tavernier were significantly less hostile than earlier writers and were sometimes openly admiring of Ottoman society and institutions. The letters from Turkey written by Lady Mary Wortley Montagu, the wife of the British Ambassador to the Ottoman Porte between 1717 and 1718, have been widely reprinted in recent years, but at the time of their publication her observations of Ottoman society and culture certainly offered an alternative viewpoint (Lockman, *Contending Visions*, pp. 64–65). Like many of the other travelers discussed here, she made the effort to learn the language and was openly scornful of earlier authors whose writings she felt were based on ignorance or gross distortion. In one letter dated June 7, 1717, she wrote:

> I see you have taken your ideas of Turkey from that worthy author Dumont, who has writ with equal ignorance and confidence. 'Tis a particular pleasure to me here to read the voyages to the Levant which are generally so far removed from the truth and so full of absurdities I am very well diverted with them. They never fail to give you an account of the women, which 'tis certain they never saw, and talking very wisely of the genius of the men, into whose company they are never admitted, and very often describe mosques which they dare not peep into.[33]

Many of the different elements found in the travel literature on the Ottoman world come together in the beautifully illustrated three-volume *Voyage pittoresque de la Grece* by the Comte de Choiseul-Gouffier, a member of the French Academy who served as the French ambassador in Istanbul between 1784 and 1791 (fig. 52). Prior to this appointment, Chosieul-Gouffier had accompanied a group of French artists and architects on a tour through the Peloponnese and the Aegean to inventory and document classical sites. The hundreds of views, sketches, and watercolors produced by members of the expedition, which included many of the leading French artists of the

FIGURE 52. M. G. F. A. Comte de Choiseul-Gouffier. *Réception de l'auteur chez Hassan Tchaousch-Oglou.*
From *Voyage pittoresque de la Grece*, Volume 1. Paris: J. J. Blaise, 1782. The O. J. Sopranos Collection

period, capture all aspects of landscape and life, from naturalistic views of rugged landscapes and craggy coastlines to market scenes featuring local villagers in traditional costumes. One of the painters on this expedition, Louis Francois Cassas, later accompanied Chosieul-Gouffier to Istanbul and was commissioned by the ambassador to travel through Anatolia and the Levant sketching and recording the classical sites of antiquity. But as the title of the volume indicates, what was depicted was a very European artistic interpretation of the landscape, one that sought to capture the sublime quality of the great ruined structures of classical antiquity and of the natural landscapes in which Greek civilization had developed. In this sense, the *Voyage pittoresque de la Grece* marks something of a turning point in European views and representations of the Ottoman world and has been seen as an important milestone in the development of French philhellenism. At the same time, alongside these idealized images, the *Voyage pittoresque* provides a remarkable inventory and catalogue with a wealth of detail on inscriptions and friezes, carefully drawn architectural site plans and elevations, charts of coastlines and harbors, and includes the first map of Istanbul based on ground surveys and measurements prepared by the French engineer Fr. Kauffer, who was attached to Chosieul-Gouffier's embassy. The first volume of Choiseul-Gouffier's *Voyage pittoresque*, which was published in 1782, was later extensively revised after the author's appointment as ambassador, and much of the original commentary on the experience and impact of Ottoman rule and the prospects for more enlightened rule and Greek liberation was removed from subsequent editions.

The emerging taste for what Murphey ("Bigots or Informed Observers?" p. 300) calls "sentimental journeying" toward the end of the eighteenth century, and the full flowering of a more romanticized travel literature on the Middle East during the nineteenth century, lie beyond the scope of this brief essay. This was a period in which European artists, poets, and novelists identified with the Romantic movement increasingly looked to the Orient for ideas and inspiration, and whose highly exoticized and often fanciful imagery captured and overwhelmed European imagination and sensibilities and fostered new forms of misunderstanding and distortion. This period also marks something of a turning point in the changing power relationship between the Ottoman state and the two dominant European powers of the period, England and France, with much more overt political and commercial interventions in the affairs of the Ottoman state. These changing political relationships are anticipated in the Comte de Volney's *Voyage en Syrie et en Égypte* published in 1787. From Napoleon's memoirs written during his exile on St. Helena we know that Volney's account of his travels in Egypt and Syria, as well as his study of the Ottoman-Russian wars, had been an important source of information in planning the French expedition to Egypt. Volney himself had discussed at some length the possibility of French administration of Egypt and the Levant as a way of achieving scientific "improvements" and advancing civilization but had concluded that such a project had little chance of success. However, as Lockman (*Contending Visions*, p. 71) has observed, "the fact that he could even entertain the idea, and that just a few years later his careful study of Egypt and Syria would be used to help make that project a reality, suggests the close connection between what contemporary Europeans were thinking and writing about the Levant and the imminent exertion of European power over it."

CARTOGRAPHY AND GEOGRAPHICAL CONSCIOUSNESS
IN THE OTTOMAN EMPIRE (1453-1730)

M. PINAR EMİRALİOĞLU
VISITING ASSISTANT PROFESSOR
HISTORY DEPARTMENT, UNIVERSITY OF PITTSBURGH

The number of cartographical depictions and narratives of geographical regions increased in the Ottoman empire between 1453 and 1730.[34] The Ottoman literati produced important works such as chronicles, *gazavatnames* (accounts of military campaigns), *shahnames* (royal histories), campaign diaries, travel books on newly conquered territories, and maps. In their accounts they described and illustrated not only the shape of the world, islands, seas, mountains, rivers, and settlements such as villages, towns, and castles, but also societies, peoples, and customs. As the second volume of the *History of Cartography* clearly demonstrates, Ottoman geographers developed a distinct Ottoman tradition in charting, military plans, and town views as early as the fifteenth century (Karamustafa, "Maps and Plans"; Soucek, "Islamic Carting in the Mediterranean"; Rogers, "Itineraries and Town Views").

This essay aims to contribute to the studies on the Ottoman geographical knowledge by historically contextualizing the major Ottoman geographical works from the early fifteenth to the eighteenth centuries. In doing so, it argues that Ottoman ruling elites and intellectuals were interested in reading, commissioning, and producing geographical works as early as the fifteenth century. They were aware of the latest geographical discoveries and the western European sources on geography. They were also competent in Islamic traditions. In their original works, they synthesized the eastern, Islamic, and western, European, traditions of geographical narratives and depictions and created the Ottoman geographical tradition. In most cases, they did not restrain themselves from adding their own observations while translating an old text or combining their eye-witness accounts with the latest knowledge on the geography of the world (Hagen, "Some Considerations"). In this way, they created their own geographical works.

This essay covers the period between 1453 and 1730. In 1453, Mehmed II (r. 1444-1446 and 1451-1481) of the Ottoman dynasty conquered Constantinople, the seat of the Byzantine empire. After the conquest, Mehmed II saw himself as the heir to the eastern Roman empire and started to entertain ideas of "world domination."[35] He also invited artists and intellectuals from Europe and allowed them to articulate his role as the universal ruler. Among these intellectuals were geographers who compiled treatises on classical geographical texts and charts of Ptolemy. Ottoman claims to universal rulership were further consolidated during the reigns of Selim I (r. 1512-1520) and Süleyman I, called "the Magnificent" (r. 1520-1566). Selim I's conquests in eastern Anatolia and at the southeastern borders of the empire started in 1514 and were followed by the annexation of Egypt, Mecca, and Medina in 1517. With these conquests the sultan not only obtained the title of the protector of the holy cities, but also confirmed that he was the *sahib-kıran* (master of an auspicious conjunction). When Selim I died, in 1520, he left an empire that reached from Anatolia to the Arab lands, including the Muslim holy places of the Hejaz and Yemen. Süleyman I inherited not only the empire, but also the title *sultan-ı heft-kişver* (the sultan of seven climes/climates). As Süleyman I consolidated the image of the "imperial ruler" with his policies, we see by the 1540s the firm development of an Ottoman imperial tradition. Süleyman's policies also brought about an expansion of central government, professionalization of bureaucracy, codification of *kanun* (imperial law), as well as its reconciliation with Islamic law (Fleischer, *Bureaucrat and Intellectual* and "Lawgiver as Messiah"). Further, it was also during his reign that the mariners of the Mediterranean found an opportunity to use their knowledge of the seas to influence the course of Ottoman expansion (Hess, "Piri Reis," p. 22). Süleyman I continued to supply the corsairs from North Africa with arms, grenades, and men. In 1533 the Ottomans established direct relations with the corsair leader, Hayreddin Barbarossa (Bostan, "Cezayir-i Bahr-ı Sefid"). During his first campaign with the Ottoman fleet, in 1534, Barbarossa took control of Tunisia, on the African coast, and of Messina and Reggio, in Sicily. After Andrea Doria, the commander of the imperial fleet of the Habsburg empire, conducted an expedition to North Africa and conquered Tunis, in 1535, the rivalry between the Ottomans and the Habsburgs intensified, especially around the North African coast, the Adriatic Sea, and the Ionian islands. As the Ottoman military campaigns continued in the Mediterranean, southeastern Europe, and Persia, Piri Re'is (d. 1554), Ali Ekber Hitayi, Ali Macar Re'is, and Mehmed Re'is enriched the collections of Ottoman geographical works. They actively charted the Mediterranean, depicted Ottoman domains, and narrated the remote corners of the world such as China and the New World.

Ottoman intellectual and imperial interest in geography and geographical works continued well into the seventeenth century. As the seventeenth century approached, the tides of battle turned in the fronts of the Mediterranean and southeastern Europe. Neither the Ottomans nor the European states were able to dominate the Mediterranean in this period, mainly because the Spanish Armada was busy in the Atlantic Ocean around the New World and the Ottomans were concerned with securing the pilgrimage routes in the eastern Mediterranean (Greene, "Resurgent Islam," pp. 325–39). The Ottoman fortunes were not any better in southeastern Europe, either. In addition to the military failures, the Ottomans also had to deal with economic crises and social upheavals in Anatolia. During this period, the Ottoman sultans stopped leading their armies in imperial campaigns and withdrew more and more to their private quarters in the palace. Grand viziers or şeyhülislams (chief jurist-councils) fulfilled the sultan's public role by forming their own households and assumed most of the sultan's executive responsibilities. Contemporary intellectuals viewed these changes in the administration of the empire and the complete halt in territorial expansion as signs of decline. Ottoman geographers such as Katib Çelebi (d. 1657), Evliya Çelebi (d. 1683), and Ebu Bekir ibn Behram el-Dimaşki were part of this milieu. They translated European atlases into Ottoman Turkish and Arabic, compiled cosmographies, and prepared voluminous travel accounts. In doing so, they criticized the corruption and disorder in the affairs of the state and simultaneously integrated the latest intellectual currents in geography into their works.

Mehmed II and the Formation of the Ottoman Imperial Capital

On May 29, 1453, Mehmed II and his army conquered Constantinople. The city had already lost its former cultural and political splendor after the Fourth Crusade in 1204. Between 1204 and 1264 the city was under the Frankish rule, during which the Crusaders sacked and almost completely destroyed the city. This period left the Byzantine empire with weakened defenses. During the fourteenth and fifteenth centuries, Ottoman expansion in the eastern Marmara region and the Balkans further obstructed the city's communication with its hinterland and weakened its defense and provisioning. Nevertheless, Constantinople still held its symbolic importance for the Ottomans. It was the capital of the eastern Roman empire and the center for the Orthodox Patriarch. It was the symbolic fortress against Islam's expansion. Before the Ottomans, Constantinople was besieged twelve times by Muslim armies. For Mehmed II, the final conquest of Constantinople was inevitable. It was the last segment of unconquered land amid the Ottoman realm.

Shortly after the conquest, Mehmed II introduced measures to rebuild and repopulate Constantinople. Muslims, Jews, and Christians from other parts of the Ottoman realm, as well as the former inhabitants of the city, were invited back and occasionally forced to settle in the city. Following the conversion of Hagia Sophia into the royal mosque, construction of the imperial mosque (the *Fatih* complex), the imperial palace (the old palace), and a tomb to commemorate Ayyub al-Ansari, a companion of the Prophet Muhammad, contributed to the reconstruction of the former Byzantine capital as an Islamic city. The new buildings also symbolized the sultan's religious and royal authority, as well as the Byzantine legacy.[36] Ottoman society ceased to be a semi-nomadic frontier. It was now a settled empire, with Constantinople as its capital. At the head of this empire was Mehmed II, who combined absolute authority with sacredness. This new style of authority found expression in the concept of "universal rulership."

Mehmed II as the Patron of Arts and Sciences: Early Beginnings of Ottoman Geography

Mehmed II's claims to universal rulership and world dominion triggered a tradition of intellectual and scientific patronage in the Ottoman palace. Istanbul eventually grew into a hub for cultural exchanges between western Europe and the Ottoman Islamic world. Artists, intellectuals, and geographers from both east and west found patronage at the palace of the sultan. Mehmed II sponsored maps and literary works on geography for two separate but interrelated reasons: intellectual curiosity about the world around him and practical assistance to his future conquests. First, he commissioned maps and geographical treatises for the intellectual activity of acquiring geographical knowledge about the world. This was certainly not a new trend in the Islamic world; since the ninth century, rulers of the Islamic states and caliphates commissioned and sponsored intellectual and scientific activities. The *Bayt al-Hikma* (School of Wisdom), founded by the Abbasid caliph al-Ma'mun (r. 813–833) in Baghdad, was a center for an enormous translation project and also served as a library for the newly translated works. Muslim scholars who took part in this unprecedented intellectual enterprise translated works on mathematics, medicine and pharmacology, and astronomy from Greek to Arabic. Soon the corpus of the extant Greek philosophical works was translated into Arabic. Therefore Mehmed II represents continuity with the tradition of intellectual and scientific patronage in the Islamic world (Brotton, *Trading Territories*, pp. 98–99). However, it is plausible to surmise that he was the first Ottoman ruler who tried to turn his capital city into a center for intellectual and artistic production. Mehmed II was familiar with legends of Alexander the Great in the Islamic texts, as well as the classical European accounts. He enjoyed listening to the classical texts of Laertius, Herodotus, Quintus Curtius, and Livy (Babinger, *Mehmed the Conqueror*, p. 112). Similarly, his library in the Topkapı Palace housed several copies of a classical geographical work, Ptolemy's *Geographia*, in Greek as well as its translations in various languages. After the conquest of Constantinople he commissioned George Amirutzes of Trebizond to compile all the regional maps of Ptolemy's *Geographia* into a single world map and encouraged him and his sons to prepare a new translation into Arabic (Karamustafa, "Maps and Plans," p. 210). George of Trebizond, a Cretan from Trebizond,[37] claims in one of his letters that he prepared a Latin translation of Ptolemy's *Almagest* and dedicated it to Mehmed II. In his second letter, in 1466, George of Trebizond wrote:

> Let no one doubt that he is by right the emperor of the Romans. For he is emperor who by right possesses the seat of the empire, but the seat of the Roman Empire is Constantinople: thus he who by right possesses this city is the emperor. But it is not from men but from God that you, thanks to your sword, have received this throne. Consequently, you are the legitimate emperor of the Romans .... And he who is and remains emperor of the Romans is also emperor of the entire earth (Babinger, *Mehmed the Conqueror*, p. 251).

Mehmed II's library also had a manuscript copy of Francesco Berlinghieri's treatise on Ptolemy's *Geographia* (fig. 3), compiled between 1464 and 1482. The work comprised four regional maps depicting Italy, Spain, France, and Palestine apart from the standard Ptolemaic maps and a commentary in verse (Brotton, *Trading Territories*, p. 90). Berlinghieri's treatise entered the Topkapı Palace Library during the reign of Bayezid II (r. 1481–1512);[38] however, the dedication on the first page of the work reads as follows: "To Mehmed of the Ottomans, illustrious prince and lord of the throne of God, emperor and merciful lord of all Asia and Greece, I dedicate this work" (Özdemir, *Ottoman Nautical Charts*, p. 52).

In addition to the intellectual curiosity about the world around him, Mehmed II encouraged geographers to draw maps for practical reasons as well. In 1479, Mehmed II commissioned an Italian painter, Gentile Bellini, to prepare his portrait. The artist stayed in Istanbul from 1479 to 1481 preparing the well-known portrait of the Ottoman sultan. Mehmed II also asked Bellini to prepare a map of Venice (Babinger, "Italian Map," pp. 8–15). Mehmed II also possessed a map of the Balkans before the conquest of Constantinople (K. Pinto, "Ways of Seeing," p. 5). Franz Babinger claims that Mehmed II himself sketched the walls of the city, the battle lines and outposts, the positions of the siege machines, batteries, and mines. He was also absorbed in an illustrated work on fortifications and siege engines (Babinger, *Mehmed the Conqueror*, p. 81). This work was, most probably, Paolo Santini da Duccio's *Tractus de re militari et machinis bellicis*; the aforementioned Balkan map is in the middle of the manuscript copy of this work.[39]

In addition to the artists from Europe and European additions to his collection of maps, the sultan's palace hosted artists and their works from Islamic lands. Mehmed II was particularly fond of Persian poetry. He himself left a *divan* (collection) of around eighty poems. He wrote almost exclusively in Turkish but the *divan* includes a few Persian poems which are imitations of *ghazels* of the Persian poet Hafiz (Babinger, *Mehmed the Conqueror*, p. 473). Mehmed II also expressed his appreciation for Persian poetry by sending gifts and annual salaries to artists from Persia and Central Asia, such as Jami (d. 1492) and Ali Shir Neva'i (d. 1501) (Babinger, *Mehmed the Conqueror*, pp. 471–73). Another significant example of influence and prestige of artists and scholars from the east and interest in maps at the Ottoman palace during the reign of Mehmed II is al-Istakhri's *Kitab al-Masalik wa al-Mamalik* [*Book of Roads and Kingdoms*].[40] Al-Istakhri was an intellectual from Fars, in southwest Iran. He is unknown apart from his *Book of Roads and Kingdoms*, which became very popular among the scholars and rulers of the Islamic world during the Middle Ages. There are many editions and abridged versions, as well as several Persian translations of the work (Miquel, "Al-Istakhri"). The earliest copy in Mehmed II's library was a gift to Mehmed II from Uzun Hasan (d. 1478), the ruler of the Aqquyunlu Turcoman tribal federation (K. Pinto, "Ways of Seeing," pp. 52–53). This copy comprised twenty-one elegant maps. Mehmed II was a patron of artists and intellectuals, both from western Europe and from Islamic lands. He was particularly interested in geography and cartography. His tradition of artistic and intellectual patronage of geographical production continued in the sixteenth century, particularly during the riegns of Selim I and Süleyman I.

Reigns of Selim I (r. 1512–1520) and Süleyman I (r. 1520–1566): Consolidation of Ottoman Geographical Consciousness

During the reign of Bayezid II (r. 1481–1512), Mehmed II's legacy of map patronage was tied to Bayezid II's quest for a stronger Ottoman navy. Realizing the need for an imperial fleet, Bayezid II summoned corsairs active around the Mediterranean and the North African coasts to his service. Before the 1480s, Ottoman maritime activities were confined to sporadic and timid attacks during which the Ottoman galleys preferred to stay close to Ottoman shores. The failures of campaigns in Rhodes (1480) and Italy (1481) signaled the need for a larger fleet that was better equipped and commanded (Hess, "Evolution," pp. 1903–04). Bayezid II appointed former corsairs Kemal Re'is (d. 1511) and Piri Re'is as naval captains. Between 1499 and 1503, the Ottoman fleet under the command of these captains achieved naval supremacy in the eastern Mediterranean (Brummett, "Overrated Adversary," p. 520). In 1502, a total of eighteen Ottoman naval ships, dispatched from Gallipoli, attacked the island of Leros and the fortresses on the island of Rhodes. The attack did not result in serious damage; however, it assured that the corsairs' activities around Rhodes were supported by the Ottoman center (Brummett, "Overrated Adversary," pp. 522–23; Vatin, *Rodos*, pp. 255–60).

As the corsairs enlivened Ottoman naval activities in the Mediterranean, they also enhanced the map collections of the Ottoman palace. Piri Re'is started his career in the eastern Mediterranean as a naval captain during the reign of Bayezid II. In 1495, the sultan summoned Piri Re'is's uncle, Kemal Re'is, to serve in the Ottoman fleet. Piri Re'is accompanied his uncle on several campaigns in the Mediterranean, esp ecially along the North African coast. After the death of Kemal Re'is in 1511, Piri Re'is withdrew to Gallipoli, where he completed his world map and the notes for his *isolario*. The career of Piri Re'is as a cartographer started during the reign of Selim I and flourished under the patronage of Süleyman I's grand vizir Ibrahim Pasha (d. 1537). The cartographer finished his world map in 1513 and presented it to Selim I just as the sultan emerged victorious in the conquest of Egypt in 1517.[41]

The eastern two-thirds of the map are lost, thus Piri Re'is's depictions of the Mediterranean, the Indian Ocean, China, and Japan are still unknown. On the extant section of the map, however, along with the Atlantic Ocean with the western coasts of Europe and Africa and the eastern coast of America, there is a long text in which Piri Re'is claims that he used five sources in drawing the Atlantic Ocean: a map by Columbus and four Portuguese charts. In this text, Piri Re'is briefly summarizes Columbus' discoveries in the New World, how Columbus interacted with the natives, the wealth of the region, and how Columbus acquired this wealth. Here, Piri Re'is states that he learned about this new region and the story of its discovery from a Spanish slave who had been with Columbus during his three journeys to the area. This world map is an excellent example of intellectual exchanges between the Ottoman and European geographers in the Mediterranean. The map is in the style of a portolan chart and incorporates the latest geographical discoveries. It is also an example of Ottoman art with its colorful ornamentations, as well as of European cartography with the several legends integrated into the map (Soucek, "Pīrī Re'īs b. Ḥādjdjī Meḥmed").

Piri Re'is finished his *isolario*, the *Kitab-ı Bahriye* [*Book of Maritime Matters*], in 1521. The *Kitab-ı Bahriye* is a geographical narrative accompanied by portolan charts of various islands and coasts of the Mediterranean. In 1526 Piri Re'is embellished the first version with colorful maps and poetry and presented it to Süleyman I.[42] The most complete copy has a total of 214 portolan charts that map 217 islands, towns, cities, and ports around the Aegean Sea, the Adriatic Sea, the central Mediterranean, the western Mediterranean, the North African coast, and the eastern Mediterranean.[43] The production of more than forty manuscript copies of the work acknowledge the importance and the popularity of the *Kitab-ı Bahriye*, not only for the Ottoman sultan, but also for a larger circle of Ottoman intellectuals.

Piri Re'is's world map and *isolario* coincide with the first Ottoman account of China. In 1516, a year before Piri Re'is presented his world map to Selim I, Ali Ekber Hitayi wrote a travel account about China called *Khitay-nameh* [*Book of China*].[44] The author prepared the work for Selim I in Persian. However, after the latter's death in 1520, the author changed its dedication and presented the work to Süleyman I. There are only four copies of the Persian version — two in Istanbul and one each in Dutch and French libraries. The *Khitay-nameh* was translated into Ottoman Turkish in 1582; this translation reached a larger audience than the original Persian version. It did not only end up in the Topkapı Palace Library, but also found its place on the shelves of several other libraries in Istanbul, Dresden, and Berlin.[45] However, the seal of possessions of these manuscripts demonstrate that the work entered Istanbul libraries only in the eighteenth and nineteenth centuries. In twenty chapters, the *Khitay-nameh* elucidates the structure of the Chinese government and the army and explains Chinese history, as well as the customs, traditions, and rules of Chinese society under the Ming dynasty (1368-1644). The work opens with a topographical description of the Arabian peninsula, Anatolia, Iran, Transoxiana, and Turkistan. The author continues with the topography of Khitay and neighboring regions. He also delineates three itineraries to reach Khitay from Ottoman domains. He specifically mentions the required travel time for an imperial army to cross the distances between two stations on each route and describes the water and food supplies, cities and towns along the routes in minute detail. The readers are regularly informed about incredible wealth and order in Khitay, as well as the conditions and number of Muslims in the area. Just like Piri Re'is, Ali Ekber Hitayi was influenced by both the eastern and western traditions of travel literature. Though he does not openly acknowledge it, Ali Ekber Hitayi used the travelogues of Marco Polo and Arab geographers such as Ibn Battuta (d. 1368), Ghiyas al-Din Naqqash, and Süleyman al-Tajir in addition to his observations (Kahle, "Islamische Quelle," p. 384).

The *Khitay-nameh* marks an Ottoman intellectual's interest in introducing far regions such as China to his audience. In a similar fashion, another Ottoman travel account from the sixteenth century introduced the New World to its readers. At the end of the sixteenth century, an anonymous Ottoman geographer compiled the first Ottoman and Muslim account of the New World, the *Tarih-i Hind-i Garbi* [*History of the India of the West*]. There are two printed editions and nineteen extant manuscript copies of the work around the world (Goodrich, *Ottoman Turks*, pp. 21-29). Among the extant manuscripts, that in the Beyazıt Library in Istanbul was prepared for the Ottoman sultan Murad III (r. 1574-1595) in 1583/1584 (ibid., p. 21). The Topkapı Palace Library also holds a manuscript copy from the late sixteenth or early seventeenth century.[46] Another copy, possibly from around 1600, is in Chicago's Newberry Library (fig. 9).[47] The autograph copy of the work is missing.

The author was perhaps an Ottoman armchair geographer or a practicing astronomer who worked with a Spanish assistant (Goodrich, *Ottoman Turks*, p. 19). According to Thomas Goodrich (ibid., pp. 20, 32-38), the latter translated the Italian editions of European works on the New World such as Francisco López de Gómara's two-volume work *Historia general de las Indias* (1552), Gonzalo Fernández de Oviedo u Valdés' *De la natural hystoria de las Indias* (1535), Peter Martyr d'Anghera (Pedro Martir d'Anghiera)'s *De orbe novo* (1511-1530), and Agustín de Zárate's *Historia del descubrimiento y conquesta del Peru* (1555).

The *Tarih-i Hind-i Garbi* reveals Ottoman intellectual curiosity about the geography, cosmography, and history of the New World. The first chapter is a short cosmography of the universe; the second chapter deals with the topography of the Mediterranean Sea and the Atlantic Ocean. In the third and final chapter, the author explicates the topography of the New World and describes its inhabitants, animals, and plants under three headings. The work is illustrated with miniature depictions of plants and animals. These depictions are also replicas of the pictures of same plants and animals in different European sources.

The large number of manuscript and printed copies of the work that survive reveals that it was diffused widely among the Ottoman literati of the late sixteenth and early seventeen centuries. The sources used to compile the work demonstrate beyond doubt the receptivity of the Ottoman literati to the flow of European knowledge and the conversation between Islamic and European sources. Among the Islamic sources that the anonymous author uses are the *'Aja'ib al-Mahlukat* [*The Wonders of Creation*] by Zakariya Qazwini (d. 1283) and *Kharidat al-'Aja'ib wa Faridat al-Ghara'ib* [*Pearls of Marvels and Unique Curiosities*] by Ibn al-Wardi (d. 1349). Translations of these works are among the earliest works in Ottoman geographical writing. They left their imprint on the *Tarih-i Hind-i Garbi*. Another area where the European sources as well as Islamic traditions influenced the Ottoman geographers was cartography. In the early modern period, Ottoman geographers actively charted the Mediterranean.

Ottoman Cartography and the Mediterranean

Already at the beginning of the sixteenth century, military conflict over control of Mediterranean lands spurred the production of the earliest Ottoman cartographic literature. The conquest of Egypt in 1517 made control of the western Mediterranean an even greater imperative for the Ottomans and brought them in direct military confrontation with the Habsburgs. Likewise, the production of *mappae mundi*, charts, and portolan atlases coincides with the long drawn-out affair of the Ottoman conquest of Cyprus in 1570. These cartographical productions bespeak a rising intellectual curiosity about the Mediterranean and also interest in employing maps as aesthetic objects among the Ottoman ruling elite. The elaborate and colorful ornamentation and detailed depictions of certain European cities such as Genoa, Venice, and Istanbul on the charts suggest that the Ottoman readers enjoyed the European art of mapmaking from their palace in Istanbul. As Ian Manners argues in his essay on European cartography, the Ottomans were active participants in intellectual currents of the early modern period as commissioners, cartographers, and audience.

Hajji Ahmed's *mappa mundi* (fig. 1) is an important example of this enterprise. As Ian Manners' essay demonstrates, this world map from 1559 is a precious example of rich cultural exchanges in the Mediterranean basin between the Ottoman world and western Europe. Hajji Ahmed's *mappa mundi* was prepared in Europe for diffusion in the Ottoman empire, particularly among the palace circles. Nevertheless, it is not the only example of a European map commissioned as a gift to an Ottoman sultan or prince who used maps and atlases during his struggles for the throne (Arbel, "Maps of the World"). The *Walters Deniz atlası* (ca. 1560) (figs. 27, 55), the atlas of Ali Macar Re'is (1567) (fig. 53), and the *Atlas-ı Hümayun* [*Imperial Atlas*] (ca. 1570) (fig. 54) are other such examples.

As the earliest of the three atlases, the *Walters Deniz atlası* features portolan charts and a world map based on European cartographic concepts (Goodrich, "Earliest Ottoman Maritime Atlas," pp. 31–35). Thomas Goodrich, who located the only copy of the atlas in the Walters Art Museum in Baltimore in 1984, has tentatively dated the *Walters Deniz atlası* to around 1560 (ibid., pp. 25–50). It was probably prepared in Italy for a readership within the Ottoman empire (Soucek, "'Ali Macar Reis Atlas,'" pp. 17–27). Although we cannot identify the original owner of the map, the good condition of the atlas and its elaborate ornamentation suggest that it was prepared for a wealthy and prestigious customer, most likely a member of the Ottoman ruling elite.

The atlas of Ali Macar Re'is, which is today preserved at the Topkapı Palace Library, dates from 1567.[48] A work of eighteen pages, it consists of six nautical charts and a world map prepared in the style of the contemporary Italian schools of Ottomano Freducci and Battista Agnese (Soucek, "Islamic Charting," p. 280). Ali Macar Re'is, an Ottoman sea captain, drew the maps of the atlas probably as a gift for a member of the Ottoman ruling elite or the sultan himself. It has also been suggested that the atlas was prepared in Italy and the place names, which were left blank, were to be filled in later by Ali Macar Re'is (Soucek, "'Ali Macar Reis Atlas,'" pp. 18–19). The world map is a copy of a large *mappa mundi* of Gastaldi dating from 1561 (Goodrich, "Unpublished Ottoman Maps," p. 99).

The *Imperial Atlas* (fig. 54) is the last and the largest of the three Ottoman atlases from the sixteenth century. Reminiscent of the previous two, it is a combination of eight portolan charts and a world map. There are differing opinions regarding the place of production of the *Imperial Atlas*. Thomas Goodrich ("Atlas-ı Hümayun") suggests that it was prepared at an Ottoman workshop located either in Istanbul, Thessalonica, or Gallipoli; he also points out that this workshop likewise produced the atlas of Ali Macar Re'is. On the other hand, Svat Soucek believes that the *Imperial Atlas* was produced in an Italian atelier, most probably in Venice. As in the atlas of Ali Macar Re'is, blanks may have been left for names to be filled in later by Ottoman cartographers (Soucek, "'Ali Macar Reis Atlas,'" p. 17).

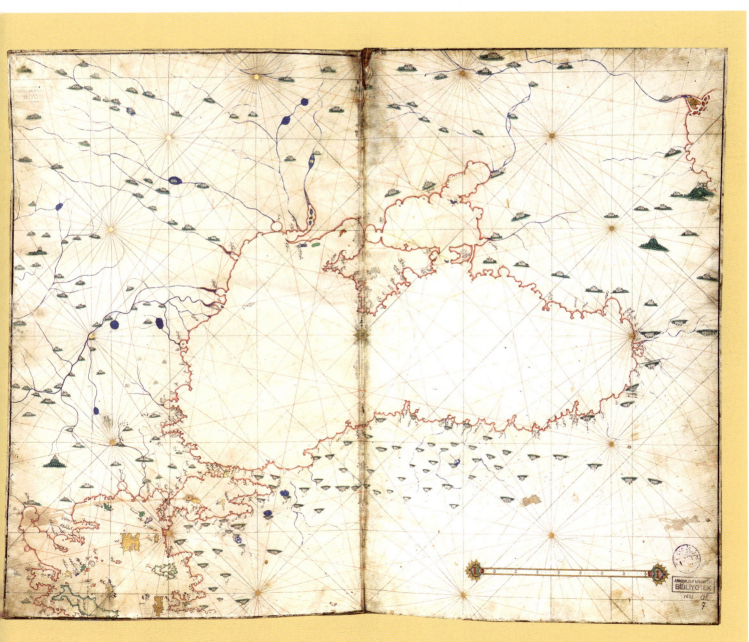

FIGURE 53. Black Sea Chart from the Ali Macar Re'is Atlas. 1567. Topkapı Palace Library, Hazine 644, folios 1b-2b. Courtesy of the Topkapı Palace Museum, Istanbul

FIGURE 54. Black Sea Chart from the *Atlas-ı Hümayun* [*Imperial Atlas*]. Folios 1b–2a. (1621).
Courtesy of the Istanbul Archaeology Museum

The first chart, common to all three atlases, is the map of the Black Sea. The Black Sea map from the *Walters Deniz atlası* (fig. 55) depicts two Ottoman cities, Bursa and Istanbul, in panoramic detail. Bursa is depicted as a generic city without any distinctive identifying features. Istanbul, the largest and most detailed of all the city panoramas in the atlas, on the other hand, is realistically portrayed. Reminiscent of earlier European depictions — such as those by Christopher Boundelmonti or Giovanni Andrea Vavassore — of the imperial center, the Istanbul panorama consists of the three major regions of the city: Galata, the *intra muros* of the old city, and the Asian coast of Üsküdar (Scutari). The artist of the work has also added minarets and domes of mosques, emphasizing the city's Islamic identity. The Hagia Irene, Hagia Sophia, the *Fatih* Mosque and the massive Süleymaniye Mosque — distinguished by a golden flag on its minaret — are easily discerned.

The Black Sea chart of Ali Macar Re'is is an exact replica of the Black Sea chart of the *Walters Deniz atlası* except that it omits the city and mountain depictions. Why do these three atlases begin with the Black Sea chart? European portolan atlases of the sixteenth century commonly place the Black Sea at the end. For example, an atlas prepared in 1544 by Battista Agnese for the abbot of the Benedictine monastery in Arras, France, features the Black Sea as the thirteenth and final map. In direct contrast to this European tradition, Ottoman atlases open with the map of the Black Sea. Is this merely because, as the use of the Arabic alphabet for the Ottoman Turkish language necessitates, Ottoman atlases open from left to right, hence the Black Sea map accidentally falls to the front when

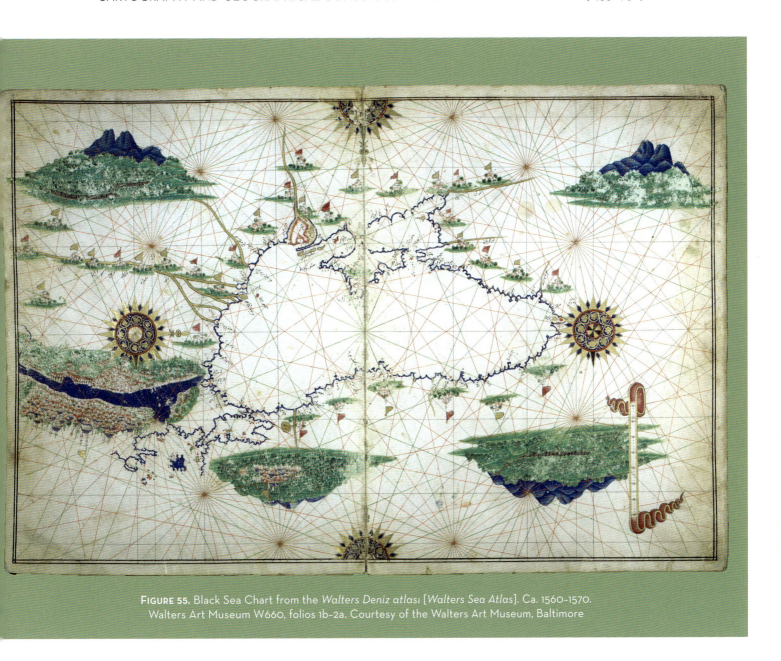

FIGURE 55. Black Sea Chart from the *Walters Deniz atlası* [*Walters Sea Atlas*]. Ca. 1560–1570.
Walters Art Museum W660, folios 1b–2a. Courtesy of the Walters Art Museum, Baltimore

it was at the end in the European context? Or could it be that the Ottomans consciously placed it at the front since the Black Sea maps contain the panoramic depiction of the Ottoman capital city of Istanbul? Since our atlases were prepared for and commissioned by the Ottoman court, it is not surprising that they begin with a map depicting the heart of the Ottoman world, the imperial capital city of Istanbul.[49]

The remaining charts in the atlases depict the eastern Mediterranean and the North African coast in a similar fashion. The atlases differ slightly from each other in their final maps. The seventh and last map of the *Walters Deniz atlası* charts the Indian Ocean (fig. 27), the eastern third of Africa, and the southern third of Asia. It has been suggested that this is "the most unusual addition … unlike any other generally known" (Soucek, "Islamic Charting," p. 283). It renders the Indian Ocean on a larger scale than the other maps in the atlas (Goodrich, "Earliest Ottoman Maritime Atlas"). It has been suggested that this map is a strong reminder of Ottoman imperial interest in the Indian Ocean in the second half of the sixteenth century (Casale, "Ottoman Age of Exploration").

Another chart that represents the Ottoman interest in the Mediterranean is the *Aegean Sea Chart* by Mehmed Re'is of Menemen (fig. 56). This nautical chart dates from 1590/1591. It remains unclear whether or not Mehmed Re'is is a fictional character like Hajji Ahmed.[50] Reminiscent of European portolan charts, Mehmed Re'is's chart encompasses the eastern Mediterranean in great detail, covering the Aegean archipelago and Aegean Sea, as well as the entire coast of the Greek peninsula from Durazzo (Albania) to the Dardanelles and the Sea of Marmara as far

FIGURE 56. Menemenli Mehmed Re'is. Aegean Sea Chart. Ca. A.H. 999 (A.D. 1590/1591). Ms. Venedig, Museo Correr, Port. 22. Courtesy of the Museo Correr, Venice

as the Bosphorus, and the Mediterranean coast of Asia Minor until the Gulf of Alexandretta. William Brice and Colin Imber suggest that Mehmed Re'is, a ship captain in the Ottoman navy, was the cartographer of this chart (Brice and Imber, "Turkish Charts," pp. 528-29). Svat Soucek suggests that Mehmed Re'is possibly acquired a blank chart from a workshop in Istanbul and later filled in the place names and even made some cartographic corrections (Soucek, "Islamic Charting," p. 283).

An anonymous portolan chart (fig. 57) dated to 1652 constitutes another possible example of an Ottoman contribution in the field of cartography in the early modern period. Today the chart is located in the manuscript department of the Bayerische Staatsbibliothek.[51] It depicts the Mediterranean as far as Mecca in the southeast; the Sea of Lut, Damascus, and Aleppo in the east; the Black Sea to the northeast; the North African coast; the Atlantic coast of Europe to the east; and the British Isles to the northwest. It is decorated with five full and five half wind roses colored in blue, black, and gold. Similar to the chart of the Aegean Sea by Mehmed Re'is, this anonymous chart was also probably produced in a workshop in Istanbul.

FIGURE 57. Anonymous Ottoman Portolan Chart. (1652). Bayerische Staatsbibliothek, Cod. turc. 431. Courtesy of the Bayerische Staatsbibliothek, Munich

Seventeenth and Eighteenth Centuries: Ottoman Cartography and Cosmography

In the seventeenth and eighteenth centuries, the Ottoman empire underwent a transformation. Territorial expansions on the eastern and western borders of the empire came to a halt. As imperial campaigns became rarer, the sultans ceased to be *ghazi*-warriors who led their armies. Instead of exercising their own authority, they delegated it to members of different political factions in Istanbul. In this period, relations with Europe also underwent a transition, which was marked by two incidents: Ottoman failure at the gates of Vienna in 1683, and the Treaty of Karlowitz in 1699. While the Europeans celebrated the first incident as the limit of Ottoman expansion in Europe, the Treaty of Karlowitz marked the first actual Ottoman withdrawal from a European territory. As Manners argues, the treaty incorporated "modern" concepts such as "territorial integrity" and "border marks" into international diplomacy. For the Ottomans, these two events changed the nature of international politics. Statesmen and policy makers in Istanbul realized that, in addition to imperial campaigns, negotiations would determine the fortunes of the Ottoman empire in Europe.

Ottoman literati followed these political developments closely. They observed these changes in international politics as signs of decline and began offering remedies (Lewis, "Ottoman Observers"). Ottoman geographers were part of this intellectual milieu in the seventeenth and eighteenth centuries. Katib Çelebi (d. 1657) and Evliya Çelebi (d. 1683), both of whom held bureaucratic and military offices during their lifetimes, articulated their concerns about the issues of statecraft in their geographical works. Katib Çelebi's works are usually considered as the "watershed in the Europeanization of Ottoman geographical literature" (Karamustafa, "Maps and Plans," p. 218). However, as this essay claims, Ottoman geographers were open to the current intellectual discussions and knowledge from Europe as early as the fifteenth century. Thus, in terms of adopting knowledge from the west, the seventeenth century represents a continuation rather than a drastic change.

Katib Çelebi was a very productive intellectual who compiled and translated numerous works on the history and geography of the Ottoman empire, the universe, and Europe. Among his well-known works is the translation of Gerardus Mercator's *Atlas minor*. Katib Çelebi acquired a copy of the *Atlas* in 1653 and started translating it with the help of Mehmed İhlas, a former French priest who had converted to Islam (Faroqhi, "Ottoman Empire," pp. 199–200; Karamustafa, "Maps and Plans," p. 218). The Topkapı Palace Library holds three manuscript copies of this translation (Goodrich, "Old Maps," pp. 125–32). The autograph copy, based on the 1621 Arnheim edition, is today in the Nuruosmaniye Library.[52] A decade after Katib Çelebi prepared his translation of *Atlas minor*, Ebu Bekir ibn Behram el-Dimaşki translated another Dutch atlas, Joan Blaeu's *Atlas maior*. Several manuscript copies of this work are kept in different libraries in Istanbul (Karamustafa, "Maps and Plans," p. 218). It is hard to claim that both of these translations reached a large circle of readers in Istanbul, however, they both bespeak a search by the Ottoman geographers for the latest knowledge in mapping the world, including China and Japan, regions that had hitherto been neglected (Faroqhi, "Ottoman Empire").

The *Cihan-nüma* [*View of the World*] by Katib Çelebi is another example of this quest. The author started compiling this voluminous cosmography in 1648. Among the sources of this first version, which covers Muslim Spain, North Africa, and the Ottoman provinces of Rumelia, Hungary, and Bosnia, was the *Tarih-i Hind-i Garbi* (Hagen, "Katip Çelebi," pp. 101–04) (fig. 9). According to Gottfried Hagen (ibid., pp. 106–10), Katib Çelebi abandoned the first edition of the *Cihan-nüma* after realizing that there was not sufficient material in Islamic geographical literature about Europe and the New World. In his second edition, Katib Çelebi relied more on European sources than on Islamic works and reduced Ottoman geographical works such as the *Tarih-i Hind-i Garbi* to second rank. Katib Çelebi died before he could finish the project. Thus, the second version of the *Cihan-nüma* starts in eastern Asia and ends at the eastern borders of the Ottoman empire (Faroqhi, "Ottoman Empire," p. 200).

In the seventeenth century, Evliya Çelebi, another Ottoman geographer, undertook a similar effort and compiled a ten-volume travel account of the Ottoman empire and its eastern and western neighbors. The author traveled to Vienna, Tabriz, Russia, Sudan, the Aegean islands, Anatolia, and Mecca as a statesman in various official and semi-official posts. Between 1630 and 1672, he collated his personal experiences during these travels with colorful stories and anecdotes in his *Seyahatname* [*Book of Travels*]. Evliya Çelebi's travelogue is the history and geography of the Ottoman world with its peripheries in the east and west (Dankoff, *Intimate Life of an Ottoman Statesman*). The *Seyahatname* starts in Istanbul and ends in Cairo, where Evliya Çelebi spent the last decade of his life. In this respect, Evliya Çelebi follows the example of Matrakçı Nasuh in placing Istanbul, the Ottoman imperial seat, at the beginning of his narrative. In his account, the author claims that he used oral sources as well as Tabari's universal history, Ottoman as well as Arabic chronicles, Persian, Hebrew, and Turkish histories, Agapios's *Kitab al-'Unvan*, an Arabic version of the *Testumonium Flavianum*, an *Atlas minor*, a "Geography," and a world map (Kreiser, "Evliya Çelebi"). Today, the reliability of Evliya Çelebi's account is in question due to the fact that he fictionalized events, used imaginary literature, and did not acknowledge most of his sources (Faroqhi, "Ottoman Empire," p. 23). Despite its flaws, the *Seyahatname* is a remarkable example of how a seventeenth-century Ottoman geographer observed the world, was conversant with sources of European and Islamic traditions, and tried to convey what he had actually seen (and what he had imagined) to his readers. Evliya Çelebi's *Seyahatname* reached a very limited audience when it was first completed. There are only eight extant manuscript copies of the work and most of these are not complete. The work was printed completely for the first time in the 1840s. It was only after this publication that it reached a larger public.

The *Seyahatname* and the *Cihan-nüma* are representative of the Ottoman world view in the seventeenth century. Both of the works endeavor to present the history and geography of the world in one complete project. Both Evliya Çelebi and Katib Çelebi were familiar with the European and Islamic sources in the field of geography and history and presented a synthesis of these sources to their readers. Their influence on the contemporary and future generation of geographers was inevitable. Evliya Çelebi's remarks on Egypt, Nubia, and Sudan appeared in 1685 on a regional map of the Nile (Karamustafa, "Maps and Plans," p. 224). Katib Çelebi's legacy in Ottoman cartography was carried to subsequent generations by Ibrahim Müterferrika (d. 1745), a Transylvanian convert to Islam who in 1727 opened the first printing press in the Ottoman empire (Berkes, "Ibrāhīm Müteferrika"). Ibrahim Müterferrika published sixteen works in his publishing house before his death, most related to geography and cartography, including the *Tarih-i Hind-i Garbi* (1730), the *Cihan-nüma* (1732), and a set of four maps. Ibrahim Müterferrika was himself a cartographer who drew a map of the Ottoman empire (Karamustafa, "Maps and Plans," p. 218). This map, based on the map of Iran from J. B. Homann's *Neuor Atlas*, is considered to be "the first modern political and economic Ottoman map" (Goodrich, "Old Maps," p. 126).

In recapitulation, during the early modern period, Ottoman literati developed an intellectual curiosity with the history and geography of the world that they lived in. Similar to their counterparts in Europe, their task was to introduce the known world to their patrons. They compiled cosmographies, wrote travelogues, and drew maps. They relied on their own observations and on the latest developments in the field of cartography and geography. In doing so, they generated a distinctively Ottoman geographical understanding of the world. The florescence of geographical works and the new Ottoman geographical consciousness in this period coincided with the rise and consolidation of Ottoman imperial claims for world dominion. The new Ottoman geographical consciousness sustained the Ottoman imperial project in two parallel ways. First, it afforded practical knowledge for further conquests. It apprised its audience of the location of historically and religiously important cities of the world. In many cases, it recounted the topography of these places as well as their history, inhabitants, flora and fauna, wealth, and economic resources. Secondly, it projected Ottoman imperial inspirations toward being a world power and assured the sultans of their magnificent personae. Most of the geographical works of the early modern Ottoman empire ended up in the palace treasury, which also served as the library. Their audience was the members of the Ottoman household and the sultan. Therefore, they reflected the world of their patrons in their works.

Ottoman geographical works, compiled during this period, were a synthesis of European and Islamic traditions. The authors and cartographers were aware of the discussions which took place in contemporary Europe, and they were also in good command of the Islamic sources. They molded Ottoman geographical knowledge by combining these two traditions. In the early modern period Istanbul, as the Ottoman imperial capital, hosted intellectuals and artists both from western Europe and the Islamic world. These intellectuals brought their own traditions and styles with them. The Ottoman geographical knowledge developed later in the sixteenth century as a synthesis of these two traditions and as a major participant in intellectual exchanges between east and west across the Mediterranean.

It is noteworthy that all examples of Ottoman geographical knowledge were compiled and circulated in manuscript form. They were available for a small circle of literati who lived either in Istanbul or in Cairo and who belonged to one or the other household of ruling elites. This is where European and Ottoman traditions of geographical works differ slightly from each other. While the first European printed maps date from the last three decades of the fifteenth century, the first printed Ottoman map is from the eighteenth century (Thrower, *Maps and Civilization*, p. 59). It was published at the printing press which was founded by Ibrahim Müterferrika and which was closed after his death. In the early modern period, the Ottomans continued participating in the development of geographical knowledge as cartographers, commissioners, and readers through the medium of the manuscript (Brotton, *Trading Territories*, p. 117). Regardless of which means they used, they were able to reach Ottoman ruling elites. They represented the world of their audience. In doing so, they constructed the imperial image and assisted the imperial project with practical information.

CATALOGUE OF EXHIBITED MAPS, ATLASES, AND TRAVEL ACCOUNTS

MAPS AND ATLASES

Date:	1482	Figure 3
Author:	Francesco di Nicolò Berlinghieri	
Title:	*Geographia*	
	Florence: Nicolas Laurentii, Alamanus	

The text, prepared by Francesco di Nicolò Berlinghieri, is a description of the world in Italian verse taken from different classical and contemporary sources; however, the regional maps follow the Ptolemaic tradition and show little difference in content from other late fifteenth-century printed Ptolemy atlases. Berlinghieri's *Geographia* is often cited as the first Ptolemy to include new maps alongside the standard Ptolemy repertoire, thus beginning the process of incorporating new geographical information derived from sources other than Ptolemy. However, this claim needs some qualification, as the four "new" maps (France, Italy, Spain, and Palestine) actually turn out to be based on previous models drawn by Pietro del Massaio perhaps as early as 1456 (Campbell, *Earliest Printed Maps*, pp. 124–25). The circumstances under which Berlinghieri inscribed a manuscript dedication of the Geographia to the Ottoman sultan, Mehmed II, are described in the chapter *European Cartographers and the Ottoman World*. Vault Ayer 6 P9 B5 1480a. The Newberry Library, Chicago (Gift of Edward E. Ayer).

Date:	1486	Figure 2
Author:	[Claudius Ptolemy]	
Title:	*Prima Asie Tabvla*	
	Geographia. Ulm: Johann Reger for Justus de Albano, 21 July 1486	

This map is from an edition of the *Geographia* printed in Ulm by Johann Reger in 1486. Judging by the number of surviving copies, the Ulm Ptolemy was the most popular of the four printed Ptolemy atlases published in the fifteenth century. It appeared first over the imprint of Lienhart Holle and was reprinted four years later by Johann Reger. The maps are based on the work of Donnus Nicolaus Germanus, who redrew earlier manuscript versions of Ptolemy's maps using a trapezoidal projection, in which both parallels and meridians are straight lines, but the meridians converge toward the poles (Campbell, *Earliest Printed Maps*, pp. 122–24). The maps in both editions repeat the same idiosyncratic reversed "N," which has been identified as the hallmark of Johannes from Armsheim near Mainz (ibid., p. 137). This map typifies the distinctive style and geographic conventions found on all Ptolemaic regional maps from the late fifteenth century. The O. J. Sopranos Collection.

Date:	1486	Figure 47
Author:	[Erhard Reuwich]	
Title:	*Rhodis*	
	Peregrinatio in Terram Sanctam. Mainz: Erhard Reuwich, 11 Feburary 1486	

Campbell (*Earliest Printed Maps*, p. 93) describes Bernhard von Breydenbach's *Peregrinatio in Terram Sanctam* as the first illustrated printed travel book. It includes a series of topographic views of Mediterranean ports and cities that are quite remarkable for their vivid and realistic portrayals of places visited by pilgrims en route to the Holy Land. These views are the work of Erhard Reuwich, an artist from Utrecht who accompanied Breydenbach on his pilgrimage in the years 1483–1484. Reuwich's regional map of Palestine and the Sinai is reproduced herein as figure 41 in the chapter *Mapping the City*. Such was the appeal of these views that they were repeatedly "borrowed" by other authors and printers, notably Hartmann Schedel, who used them in the *Liber Chronicarum*, and Braun and Hogenberg, who recycled several of the images and elements of the map of Palestine in their *Civitates Orbis Terrarum*, published nearly one hundred years after Breydenbach's original journey. The O. J. Sopranos Collection.

Date: 1493   Figure 40
Author: Hartmann Schedel
Title: Constantinopolis
           Liber Chronicarum. Nuremberg: Anton Koberger

The *Liber Chronicarum* (usually identified as the *Nuremberg Chronicle*), in which this bird's-eye view of Constantinople appears, is one of the most richly illustrated printed books of the fifteenth century. In all, over 600 woodcuts appear in the text, including representations of emperors, kings, saints, and martyrs, as well as two maps and numerous topographic views of cities. The view of Constantinople is repeated in a number of slight variations throughout the text. The double folio view on display is the most detailed, with the artist showing the city's double land walls with their massive crenellated towers; sea defenses, including the chain across the entrance to the Golden Horn; the church of Hagia Sophia; and other major landmarks and monuments in such a way as to render the city recognizable; conspicuously displayed over the gateways is the crest of the "imperator gloriolus," the crown and double-headed eagle of Byzantium, reinforcing the sense that this is a city that has not yet been lost to Christianity. Other woodcuts of Constantinople scattered through the text are clearly derived from this model, but are cruder in execution and omit a number of features; moreover they appear in sections of the text that have no relationship to the history of the city. The topographic views in the *Liber Chronicarum* are therefore an intriguing combination of imaginary images with only minimal links to the real world, and, where information was available to the artist, more realistic representations of place using new ideas about perspective; in this sense the *Liber Chronicarum* stands at a transition point between medieval and Renaissance ways of seeing and mapping the world. The O. J. Sopranos Collection.

Date: 1511   Figure 4
Author: Bernardus Sylvanus
Title: *Prima Asiae Tabvla* and (verso) sections of *Secvnda Asiae Tabvla* and *Qvarta Africae Tabvla*
           Clavdii Ptolemaei Alexandrini Liber geographiae .... Venetiis per Iacobum Pentium de leucho Anno
           domini M.D.XI

Sylvanus' edition of the *Geographia*, entitled *Clavdii Ptolemaei Alexandrini Liber geographiae ...*, in which this map appeared, was one of the first efforts to update the standard Ptolemaic maps with more current information. Since most changes involve coastlines and coastal features, it seems probable that Sylvanus took much of the "new" information from portolan charts. This was also the first Ptolemy atlas to use two-color printing (red and black) and, unusual for this period, has maps printed on both sides of the leaf. Each map in the atlas was printed using two woodblocks with the result that there is a slight gap along the gutter of the atlas (Karrow, *Mapmakers*, pp. 522-24). The O. J. Sopranos Collection.

Date: 1541   Figure 5
Author: Lorenz Fries
Title: *Tabula noua Asiæ minoris*
           Ptolemaei Alexandrini Clavdii geographicae ... Excudebat Gaspar Treschel Viennae M.D.XLI

The woodblocks used for the maps in Fries' 1541 Ptolemy atlas had been used in several earlier printings (Strasburg 1522 and 1525; Lyons 1535, reprinted in 1541). In a note in the 1522 edition, Fries acknowledges that he had simplified and reduced maps originally drawn by Martin Waldseemüller (Karrow, *Mapmakers*, pp. 194-96). The text for the 1535 edition was prepared by Michel de Villeneuve (better known to us as Michael Servetus). One of the charges against Servetus at the time of his interrogation by the Inquisition was that he had described Palestine as being largely infertile. Karrow (ibid., p. 199) notes that this statement actually originated in Fries' 1522 edition. Escaping from imprisonment, Servetus was detained in Geneva, where he was brought to trial and condemned largely on the basis of testimony by John Calvin. At the time of his execution, in 1553, many of Servetus' works, including copies of his Ptolemy, were burned. The O. J. Sopranos Collection.

Date:	1559 & 1561	Figure 7
Author:	Giacomo Gastaldi	
Title:	*Il disegno della prima parte del Asia …* and *Il disegno della seconda parte dell'Asia …*	
	Venetia [Venice] 1559 and Venetia [Venice] 1561	

Gastaldi's large three-part map of Asia was regarded as the definitive map of the continent until well into the seventeenth century. The first section, *Il disegno della prima parte del Asia …*, is on two sheets covering Turkey and the eastern Mediterranean and appeared in 1559; the second section, *Il disegno della seconda parte del Asia …*, covers the area between the Red Sea and India and appeared in 1561. The authority of the map derived in large part from the inclusion of new geographic information taken from the direct observations of travelers. In moving away from reliance on classical texts and sources, Gastaldi benefited from his close friendship with Giovanni Battista Ramusio who, as secretary to the Venetian Senate and, after 1553, to the Council of Ten, had access to the latest geographical information reaching Venice. All the late sixteenth- and early seventeenth-century maps of the Ottoman empire, including those by Ortelius and de Jode on display in the exhibit, as well as those appearing in Mercator-Hondius-Jansson and Blaeu world atlases, are based on Gastaldi's maps and sources. Novacco 4F 373 and Novacco 4F 386. The Newberry Library, Chicago (Franco Novacco Map Collection).

Date:	[1559] 1795	Figure 1
Author:	[Hajji Ahmed]	
Title:	[*A Complete and Perfect Map Describing the Whole World*]	

This large woodcut map of the world on ten sheets using a cordiform ("heart-shaped") projection was prepared in Venice ca. 1559; however, the blocks were confiscated by the Venetian authorities and were apparently forgotten until 1795, when twenty-four impressions were made by the official printer for Simone Assemani, a professor of oriental languages at the University of Padua (Karrow, *Mapmakers*, p. 172). No copies of the map are known from the sixteenth century. The circumstances surrounding the preparation of this map, the sources of information used by the mapmaker, and the likelihood that the pseudonym Hajji Ahmed was actually part of a wider conceit by the Venetian publisher Giustinian to promote the map as a commercial venture among Ottoman and perhaps even Safavid clients are discussed in the introductory essay, *European Cartographers and the Ottoman World*. Novacco 8F 011. The Newberry Library, Chicago (Franco Novacco Map Collection).

Date:	ca. 1560	Figures 27 and 55
Author:	—	
Title:	*Walters Deniz atlası* [*Walters Sea Atlas*]	

The *Walters Deniz atlası* illustrates the Ottoman contribution to the Mediterranean tradition of sea charting. In addition to the usual series of portolan charts of the Mediterranean and Black seas, the *Deniz atlası* includes an unusual chart of the Indian Ocean, something that was not replicated in other sea atlases of the period. There is also a world map drawn using an oval projection that Soucek ("Islamic Charting in the Mediterranean," pp. 282–83) suggests is similar to those appearing in portolan atlases drawn by the Venetian mapmaker Battista Agnese. However, the atlas was almost certainly produced in Istanbul, and the Ottoman authorship is clear from the legends and the reverse sequencing of the maps. Goodrich (1986) dates the atlas to ca. 1560 and concludes that it was probably prepared as a presentation copy. Walters Art Museum W660, folios 1b–2a and 7b-8a. The Walters Art Museum, Baltimore.

Date: 1568   Figure 25
Author: Domenico Oliva
Title: Manuscript Portolan Chart of the Mediterranean and Black Seas

Although this is a late example of a portolan chart, it illustrates many of the features of this tradition of charting which was rooted in first-hand experience of the Mediterranean Sea. The accuracy of the portolan charts with respect to the shape of the Mediterranean is quite remarkable, and their mapping of coastlines was far superior to anything achieved in Ptolemaic maps. Like other portolans, the Oliva chart is drawn on vellum and hand colored; in this instance, the "neck" of the skin carries a depiction of the crucifixion of Christ, intended to serve as protection for the mariner. Other shared characteristics are the interconnecting rhumb lines, the orderly sequence of place names that follow the coastline, and the exaggerated attention given to those coastal features — sandbanks, headlands, shoals, rocks, and safe anchorages — which were of greatest importance to the mariner. Vault Oversize Ayer MS map 16. The Newberry Library, Chicago (Gift of Edward E. Ayer).

Date: [1579] 1602   Figure 10
Author: Abraham Ortelius
Title: *Tvrcici Imperii Descriptio*
             Theatrum Orbis Terrarum. [Antwerp]

The first edition of Ortelius' *Theatrum Orbis Terrarum*, published in May, 1570, contained seventy maps (including *Tvrcici Imperii Descriptio*) and listed eighty-seven cartographers as sources for the atlas (Karrow, *Mapmakers*). According to van den Broecke (*Ortelius Atlas Maps*), there were two slightly different versions of the map of the Ottoman empire. The map in the exhibit (which appeared in the 1602 German edition) is the second rendition; this first appeared in a 1579 Latin edition of the *Theatrum* and was used in all subsequent editions. The later plate is identifiable by a more ornate cartouche, but the substantive content of the map remained unchanged. In compiling the map, Ortelius drew from his earlier map of Asia (1567), which was itself based on Gastaldi's map of Asia (1559–1561). The O. J. Sopranos Collection.

Date: [1572–1617]   Figures 32–35 and 38
Author: Georg Braun and Frans Hogenberg
Title: *Civitates Orbis Terrarum*
             Antverpiae Apud Philipum Gallaeum, et Coloniae Apud Auctores, 1572

The six-volume city atlas edited by Braun, with plates engraved, for the most part, by Hogenberg, appeared between 1572 and 1617. Although the entire work is usually referred to as the *Civitates Orbis Terrarum*, this title only appears in Book I. The authors worked from existing models as well as from original sketches and views produced for the atlas by contributing artists, notably Georg Hoefnagel. Initially more modestly conceived, Braun, in the foreword to Book II, invited individuals who felt slighted that their native towns had been omitted to supply materials for inclusion in future works; the resulting response greatly expanded the scope of the undertaking although the later volumes are dominated by views of Dutch and German towns. The appeal of the atlas can be judged from the frequent number of reprintings and translations; after the deaths of the editors, the plates were acquired by the map publisher Jan Jansson, who re-used them with additional new plates in his own six-volume *Illustriorum ... urbium tabulae* (1657), and later by Jannsonius van Waesberghe, Frederick de Witt, and Peter van der Aa, all of whom used the plates in their own multi-volume city atlases. In the middle of the eighteenth century they were in the hands of the Dutch publishing house of Cóvens & Mortier, who "used them until they were worn out" (Skelton, "Background Notes," p. xxi).

    The plates were also used to supply a parallel market for single-sheet engravings, and the exhibit includes four views from the O. J. Sopranos Collection that appeared in Books I and II of the *Civitates*: *Byzantivm nunc Constantinopolis*; *Cairos, qvae olim Babylon Aegypti maxima vrbs*; *Damascvs, vrbs nobilissima ad Libanum montem, Totius Sÿriæ Metropolis*; and *Alexandria, vetustissimum Ægÿpti emporium ....* Also included is a view of Tunis, *Tvnes, Oppidvm Barbarie ...,* on loan from The University of Chicago Library, Special Collections Research Center.

Date: 1578   Figure 10

Author: Gerard de Jode

Title: *Tvrcia Tvrcicive Imperii seu Solij mannorum regni pleraque pars, nunc recens summa fide ac industria elucubrata*
Specvlvm Orbis Terrarvm. Antwerp

De Jode's *Specvlvm Orbis Terrarvm*, in which this map appeared, was published in Antwerp in 1578. De Jode was a printer and map publisher who was admitted to the Guild of St. Luke (the painter's guild) in Antwerp as an "illuminator of maps" in 1547, the same year as Ortelius (Karrow, *Mapmakers*, p. 1). Although de Jode was the publisher of Ortelius' first map, the relationship appears to have become strained and Ortelius does not include de Jode's name in the *Catalogus Auctorum* in the *Theatrum*. Ortelius' name is likewise missing from the list of authorities cited by de Jode for the *Specvlvm*. Whether or not this estrangement was due to professional rivalry over plans to produce an atlas is unclear, but Skelton ("Background Notes," p. vi) suggests that there is strong evidence to believe that Ortelius used his influence and connections to obstruct and delay the licensing and production of de Jode's atlas. Like his rival, de Jode relied heavily on prototypes as models, and his maps of Asia and the Ottoman empire are based on Gastaldi's earlier work. The O. J. Sopranos Collection.

Date: 1583   Figure 28

Author: Joan Martines

Title: [*Manuscript Portolan Atlas of the Mediterranean and the African Coast*]

This beautifully illuminated late sixteenth-century portolan atlas comprises five maps drawn on vellum and hand colored. In addition to two charts covering the eastern and western Mediterranean, there are charts of northwestern Africa, the coast of west Africa between Mauritania and the Cape of Good Hope, and the British Isles and northwest Europe, illustrating the extension of the portolan tradition to new regions outside the core Mediterranean. Clearly, atlases such as this one were intended as presentation copies, rather than for use at sea. On the verso of the last chart appears a note tracing the chart's ownership; this includes a 1595 inscription signed by W. L. Burghly(?) (identified as William Cecil, Lord Burghley, who served as secretary and treasurer to Elizabeth I), noting that he was given the atlas by Charles Lord Howard of Effingham, the English Lord Admiral at the time of the Spanish Armada. Vault folio Ayre MS map 21. The Newberry Library, Chicago (Gift of Edward E. Ayer).

Date: 1595   Figure 29

Author: Willem Barentsz

Title: *Thalassografica Tabula totius Maris Mediterranei*
Amsterdam

Barentsz' sea chart of the Mediterranean follows the style and format of the earlier portolan charts. However, by the end of the sixteenth century, the Dutch had taken the lead in nautical cartography and their printed sea atlases (waggoners) and navigational charts, incorporating additional hydrographic data derived from direct soundings and coastal surveys, were widely reprinted and copied. Barentsz' *Caertboeck van de Midlandtsche Zee* (1595) was the first to extend the Dutch approach to sea charting into the Mediterranean (Whitfield, *Charting of the Oceans*). The O. J. Sopranos Collection.

Date: 1596   Figure 31

Author: [Jan Huygen van Linschoten]

Title: *Deliniatuur in hac tabula, Oræ maritimæ Abexiæ, freti Meccani, al Maris Rubri, Arabiæ ...,*
Itinerario, Voyage ofte Schipvaert van Jan Huygen van Linschoten naar Oost-ofte Portugalis
Indien. Amsterdam, Cornelis Claesz

Linschoten's knowledge of the sea routes around Africa to India and the East Indies (derived in large part from the rutters [sea journals] of Portuguese pilots), and his familiarity with local and regional conditions of trade as a result of the eight years he spent in Goa, was an important element in successful Dutch commercial expansion into the East Indies trade. Linschoten's description of India and account of his experience appeared in 1596 under the title *Itinerario, voyage ofte schipvaert van Jan Huygen van Linschoten naar Oost-ofte Portugalis Indien.* The maps, drawn by Henricus Langene, were far more accurate, particularly in their depiction of coastlines, than anything found in the work of Gastaldi or Ortelius, and the information was quickly picked up and incorporated into the regional maps appearing in Mercator-Hondius-Jansson and Blaeu world atlases. The O. J. Sopranos Collection.

Date: [ca. 1600]   Figure 9

Author: —

Title: *Tarih-i Hind-i Garbi* [*History of the India of the West*]

This is an unsigned manuscript copy of the *Tarih-i Hindi-i Garbi* [*A History of the India of the West*] that was originally written around 1580. According to Goodrich ("Ottoman Americana"), the Newberry copy, entitled *Tarih-i Yeni Dünya* [*History of the New World*], is probably closest to the original. The earliest surviving copy of the manuscript is dated 1583/1584 and was a presentation copy prepared for Sultan Murad III. The book is divided into three parts: the first chapter summarizes traditional Islamic cosmology and geography with information added by the author about the New World and Magellan's circumnavigation of the globe; the second chapter includes information about the coastlines of the Atlantic Ocean; while the third and most extensive chapter is a history of the exploration and conquest of America from 1492 to 1552, together with descriptive materials on geography, natural history, and anthropology. Thirteen color miniatures illustrate textual descriptions of American flora and fauna. Goodrich identifies four Spanish authorities from whom the anonymous Ottoman author of the manuscript has drawn information. There is some evidence suggesting that the Ottoman compiler did not have access to the original texts, but worked from Ramusio's *Delle Navigationi et Viaggi.* The Newberry copy includes three double-page maps, oriented with the south at the top; the rectangular world map displayed appears to be a copy of one by Gastaldi that first appeared in a 1548 Venetian edition of Ptolemy's *Geographia.* Ayer MS 612. The Newberry Library, Chicago (Gift of Edward E. Ayer).

Date: [1635] 1680?   Figure 12

Author: Frederick de Witt

Title: *Tvrcicvm Imperivm*
Atlas maior. Amsterdam

Frederick de Witt was one of the most successful map publishers in The Netherlands in the second half of the seventeenth century. His publishing firm produced a wide range of world atlases, sea charts, wall maps, globes, and city views. De Witt engraved maps in his own right, but he also acquired at auction plates of other publishers. The map of the Ottoman empire in the exhibit is from a 1680 edition of de Witt's *Atlas maior,* but the information is largely derived from a map originally prepared by Willem and Joan Blaeu for their *Novus Atlas* (1635), which was frequently reprinted in later editions of that atlas. De Witt's stock of maps and copper plates was acquired in the early eighteenth century by Pieter Mortier and editions of de Witt's atlases continued to be issued by the Cóvens & Mortier publishing house well into the eighteenth century. The O. J. Sopranos Collection.

Date: 1641   Figure 42
Author: Matthäus Merian
Title: *Constantinopolis. Constantinopolitanæ vrbis effigies ad vivum expressa, qvam Tvrcæ stampoldam vocant*
       Johannes Angelius von Werdenhagen, *De Rebuspublicus Hanseaticis.* Frankfurt

Merian was a prolific engraver of city plans and views, a genre of topographic mapping that was extremely popular in the sixteenth and seventeenth centuries. Merian's sweeping panoramic view of Constantinople and the Golden Horn from a point above Pera reflects the artistic concern with showing the city realistically, as it would appear to the eye of the traveler. The sailing ships and the figures in the foreground contribute to the sense of place and the lifelike quality of the image, contrasting the exact spatial accuracy of a city plan. The view appears in an edition of Johannes Angelius von Werdenhagen's *De Rebuspublicus Hanseaticis*, published by Merian in 1641, in Frankfurt. Merian (and after his death, his son, Matthäus Merian the Younger) were also involved in the production of a twenty-two-volume set of city plans, topographical views, and regional maps published under the title *Theatrum Europaeum* (1635–1738); Merian's engraving of Constantinople was included in Volume 16 (1717). Many later panoramic views (for example, by Frederick de Witt, 1680) are reiterations of Merian's work. The O. J. Sopranos Collection.

Date: [1652]   Figure 20
Author: Nicolas Sanson
Title: *Les Estats de l'Empire des Turqs en Asie*
       Paris: Chez Pierre Mariette ...

Sanson's maps and innovative geographical tables were widely seen by his contemporaries as setting new standards of "scientific" accuracy. His approach reveals a preoccupation, almost an obsession, with organizing and mapping geographical information (boundaries, administrative units, settlements) according to hierarchies. The continued celebration of Sanson's work, and what Pastoureau (*Nicolas Sanson d'Abbeville*, p. 43) describes as "orchestrated eulogies" by his heirs, helped to sustain Sanson's reputation over many generations, but one result was that his maps, laboriously reworked and corrected, remained in circulation right up to the eve of the French Revolution. Sanson was one of the first cartographers to differentiate cartographically between "Turkey in Europe" and "Turkey in Asia." The map in the exhibit was engraved in 1652; it circulated as a single-sheet map and was included in the first edition of Sanson's *Cartes generales de toutes parties du monde ....* (Paris: Pierre Mariette, 1658). The O. J. Sopranos Collection.

Date: 1664   Figure 14
Author: Pierre du Val
Title: *Carte de L'Empire des Tvrcs et de ses confins*
       Paris

Pierre du Val was Nicolas Sanson's son-in-law. He published a wide range of military and historical maps in his own right, as well as world atlases which borrowed heavily from Sanson's published work. This map is from a 1664 edition of du Val's *Le Monde, ou, La Geographie universelle contenant les descriptions, les cartes, & le blazon de principaux pays du monde*, published in Paris. The O. J. Sopranos Collection.

		Not illustrated
Date:	1664	
Author:	Francisco Maria Levanto	
Title:	*Prima Parte dello Specchio del Mare*	
	Genoa: Gerolamo Marino & Benedetto Celle	

Levanto was a Genoese ship captain with several decades experience of navigating the Mediterranean. His atlas follows in the tradition of earlier portolan charts prepared not just for mariners, but frequently by mariners. The *Specchio* also connects the Mediterranean charting tradition with Dutch advances in hydrographic mapping from the early seventeenth century. Levanto worked from Dutch models, although he notes in the preface that his charts are subject to different compass variations. According to Koeman (*Atlantes Neerlandici*, vol. 4, p. 217), the atlas is a direct copy of the Mediterranean volume of Pieter Goos' *Zee-Spiegel*. The atlas includes twenty-four double-page maps covering the Mediterranean from Gibralter to Alexandria, with additional text on navigational aides and profile views of coastlines with landmarks observable from the sea. Levanto's charts were widely copied and appropriated, and strongly influenced the development of maritime cartography in Italy during the second half of the seventeenth century. The O. J. Sopranos Collection.

		Not illustrated
Date:	1676	
Author:	Hendrick Doncker	
Title:	*Vera dichiaratione del Mare del Archipelago con tutti soi insuli, porti, spiaggie, e secci &c.*	
	Portatato in luce da Pietro Silvestro Valck	
	Amsterdam: [H. Doncker]	

Hendrick Doncker was a successful chart-seller and publisher of sea atlases in Amsterdam at a time when the Dutch still dominated nautical map production. Many of his sea atlases and pilot guides were jointly produced with Pieter Goos and Anthonie Jacobsz and were reprinted well into the eighteenth century. This is an unusual and previously unrecorded Italian-language edition of Doncker's chartbook of the Aegean and eastern Mediterranean. That the atlas follows in the portolan tradition is very clear in the compass roses, rhumb lines, and alignment of place names along the coastline, but Doncker incorporates a latitudinal grid and provides more detailed information about reefs, estuaries, and harbors, while the charts of ports and anchorages include depth soundings. In contrast to some of the presentational sea atlases in the exhibit, this was intended for practical use, and the charts were originally backed with an extra sheet of heavy paper for durability at sea. The O. J. Sopranos Collection.

		Figure 30
Date:	[1694] 1711	
Author:	Romeijn de Hooghe	
Title:	*Carte Nouvelle de la Mer Mediterranee où sont Exactement Remarqués tous les Ports, Golfes,*	
	Rochers, Bancs de Sable &c. a l'usage des Armées, du Roy de la Grande Bretagne ...	
	Amsterdam: Chez J. Cóvens & C. Mortier	

Romeijn de Hooghe's chart of the Mediterranean, with surrounding views of ports and harbors from Cadiz to Constantinople and an elaborate cartouche depicting Neptune and Athena, is an outstanding example of Dutch map art from the late sixteenth century. This was one of nine charts that de Hooghe engraved for a maritime atlas published in Amsterdam by Pieter Mortier in 1694. The dedication in the cartouche to the King of England is to William of Orange, at that time the crowned head of both The Netherlands, and, through his marriage to Mary Stuart, of Great Britain. In fact, Mortier's atlas was pirated from a French collection of sea charts, *Le Neptune François*, published in Paris under royal privilege in 1693. The map in the exhibit is from a later printing as indicated by the imprint of J. Cóvens & C. Mortier, who inherited the estate of Pieter Mortier at the time of his death in 1711. Clearly, such atlases were intended for the library or salon, rather than for use at sea (Whitfield, *Charting of the Oceans*, p. 87). The O. J. Sopranos Collection.

Date: [1701] 1745   Figure 16
Author: Guillaume de L'Isle
Title: *Carte de la Turquie de l'Arabie et de la Perse. Dressée sur les Memoires les plus recens rectifiez par les Observations de M^{rs}. de l'Academie Roy^{le} des Sciences*
                Amsterdam: Chez Iean Cóvens & Corneille Mortier

De L'Isle's map of Turkey, Arabia, and Persia was originally engraved in 1701 and published in Paris; it was sold as a single-sheet map and was reproduced in several atlases, including de L'Isle's *Atlas de Géographie* (1715). The copy on display is from a 1745 edition of the *Atlas Nouveau* published in Amsterdam by Jean Cóvens and Corneille Mortier with an added superscript, *Tabula Nova Imperii Turcarum, Arabum et Persarum*. De L'Isle was the foremost French cartographer of the early eighteenth century; his critical approach to mapping and his training in mathematics and astronomy as a student of J. D. Cassini were very much in keeping with what was seen as a more scientific approach to cartography in the French Enlightenment period. However, for the content of his regional maps, he remained largely dependent on the accounts and observations of "non-scientific" travelers. Such was de L'Isle's reputation that his maps continued to be reprinted long after his death in 1726. According to Koeman (*Atlantes Neerlandici*), de L'Isle's maps were re-engraved by Cóvens & Mortier for editions of their *Atlas Nouveau*, published between 1730 and 1757. The O. J. Sopranos Collection.

Date: 1717   Figure 19
Author: Guillaume de L'Isle
Title: *Carte particuliere de la Hongrie, de la Transilvanie, de la Croatie, et de la Sclavonie, Dressée sur les Observations de M^r. le Comte Marsilli et sur plusieurs autre Memoires.* Paris: Chez l'auteur sur le quai de l'Horloge ...

Luigi Ferdinando Marsigli served as an "engineer" officer in the Habsburg army during the campaigns that preceded the Treaty of Karlowitz (1699). For much of this time he was involved in conducting detailed surveys of the Danube below Buda; this included assessment of possible frontiers in the event of a future peace and preparation of topographic maps, in the course of which he corresponded with Cassini in France about ways of ensuring the accuracy of his calculations (Stoye, *Marsigli's Europe*). He was appointed by Leopold I as the Habsburg boundary commissioner following the signing of the Treaty of Karlowitz, and with his Ottoman counterpart spent nearly two years demarcating the new frontier on the ground. The maps of the boundary commission were prepared by a German surveyor, Johann Müller, who had previously served as Marsigli's secretary and draughtsman. Marsigli was later cashiered from the Habsburg army and traveled to Paris in search of French support and patronage. As Krokar (*Ottoman Presence*) notes, de L'Isle's map of Hungary, printed in Paris in 1717, was one of the first maps to correctly show the course of the Danube and was clearly based on information provided by Marsigli. A similar map had previously been published in 1709 in a limited German edition under Müller's name, and whether de L'Isle copied this map or drew directly from Marsigli's field notes and detailed sketches is unclear; however, since de L'Isle was a protégé of Cassini and involved in the French national survey, a direct connection is not impossible, particularly in light of Marsigli's presence in Paris. Sack Map 4f G6500 1717 .L5. The Newberry Library, Chicago (John Gabriel Sack Map Collection).

Date: 1720   Figure 15
Author: Herman Moll
Title: *The Turkish Empire in Europe, Asia and Africa, Dividid into all its Governments, together with the other Territories that are Tributary to it, as also the Dominions of ye Emperor of Marocco. According to the Newest and most Exact Observations*

Moll was the leading English cartographer of the first half of the eighteenth century. Of German origin, he appears to have moved to England around the time of the Hanoverian succession and enjoyed a reputation as a skilled and accomplished engraver of copperplate (Reinhartz, *Cartographer and Literati*). His output was prolific and included world geographies, globes, and atlases, as well as individual sheet maps and charts. He was extremely successful as a businessman, but his handsomely engraved maps are essentially compilations of information taken from other cartographers. Reinhartz (ibid., p. 39) comments that Moll could not resist airing his theories and prejudices in long notes scattered over the map. This map of the Turkish empire was originally prepared for *The World Described*, which appeared in numerous editions between 1715 and 1754, and is based on works by de L'Isle. After Moll's death his plates passed to his partner, Thomas Bowles, and then to Bowles' son, and remained in use, often uncorrected, for another half century. The O. J. Sopranos Collection.

Date:	1764/1765	Figure 37
Author:	Ahmad Ardarumi (Ahmad of Erzurum?)	
Title:	*Kitab dala'il al-khairat wa shawariq al-anwar fi dkikh al-salat 'ala al-nabiyy al-mukhtar*	

This manuscript represents the well-established Islamic tradition of illuminating pilgrimage scrolls. The the main subject of these illustrations are the principal shrines visited in the course of the hajj. Some were intended to post-humously commemorate a proxy pilgrimage; they were also adapted to illustrate verse guides for those performing the hajj (Rogers, "Itineraries and Town Views," p. 244). Similar devotional books circulated fairly widely in the Ottoman world during the seventeenth and eighteenth centuries and continued to be produced into the nineteenth century. A common feature of these books were bird's-eye views of the cities of Mecca and Medina. This copy, dated to 1764/1765, was prepared by Ahmad Ardarumi (Ahmad of Erzurum) from an original fifteenth-century manuscript by al-Jazuli al Simiali. OIM A12048. The Oriental Institute, The University of Chicago.

Date:	1822	Figure 43
Author:	Fr. Kauffer	
Title:	*Voyage pittoresque de la Grece.* Paris: J. J. Blaise	

This plan of Constantinople marks something of a watershed in the mapping of the city by European cartographers. Although the mathematical basis for constructing the ground plan, in which distances and spatial relationships are shown accurately and according to scale, and the surveying instruments that made its construction possible, had been perfected well before the end of the sixteenth century, Kauffer's plan is the first to apply these methods to Istanbul. Kauffer was an engineer attached to the staff of the French Embassy, and his plan was reproduced in the *Voyage pittoresque de la Grece* by the Comte de Choiseul-Gouffier, a member of the French Academy who served as the French ambassador in Istanbul between 1784 and 1791. The O. J. Sopranos Collection.

Date:	1803	Figure 22
Author:	[William Faden]	
Title:	*[The Western Mediterranean Sea]* from *Cedid atlas tercümesi [Translation of the New Atlas]* Üsküdar [Istanbul]: Tab'hane-yi Humayun'da	

This map is from the *Cedid atlas tercümesi*, a world atlas printed in Istanbul in 1803 for the Ottoman Military Engineering School. It was produced to provide students and faculty in the new school with an introduction to contemporary geographic and cartographic practices in western Europe, and was linked to late eighteenth- and early nineteenth-century efforts to transform and modernize the Ottoman military. All the maps in the atlas were taken from an edition of William Faden's *General Atlas*, which had been acquired by Mahmud Ra'if Efendi when he was private secretary to the Ottoman ambassador in London. The Ottoman translation was prepared by Yakovaki Efendi and the maps re-engraved under the direction of Abdurrahman Efendi. Only fifty copies of the atlas were printed, including a presentation copy for Sultan Selim III. The Newberry copy also includes a geographical introduction by Mahmud Ra'if Efendi, which originally appeared as a separate work under the title *Ucaletu'l-Coğrafiye* [*Handbook of Geography*], in 1804. Vault Baskes + G1019 T2 1803. The Newberry Library, Chicago (Gift of Roger S. Baskes).

Date: [1816?]   Figure 51
Author: William Faden
Title: [*General Atlas: A Collection of Large-Scale Maps and Charts of All Parts of the World by Various Cartographers and Publishers*]
            London: William Faden, 1775–1816

This collection of maps, published by William Faden ca. 1816, includes "A New Map of Arabia, Divided into Its Several Regions and Districts, From Mon^sr. d'Anville, Geographer to the most Christian King, with Additions and Improvements from M^r. Niebuhr." This map carries the imprint of Laurie & Whittle and is dated 1794. The nature and impact of scientific exploration, as exemplified in the Royal Danish Expedition to Arabia, undertaken between 1761 and 1767, of whom Carsten Niebuhr was the sole survivor, is discussed in the chapter *Through Travelers' Eyes.* Niebuhr's mapping of Yemen and interior Arabia remained the standard source for cartographers until well into the twentieth century. Ayer 135 G32 1775, v. 2. The Newberry Library, Chicago (Gift of Edward E. Ayer).

TRAVEL ACCOUNTS

Christopher Buondelmonti, fl. 1420   Figure 46
Liber insularum archipelagi ...

The original manuscript was most likely completed sometime after 1418. It was widely copied in the fifteenth and first half of the sixteenth century, and these copies exhibit wide differences in content and style. Included in the exhibit is the first printed edition prepared by G. R. L. von Sinner, *Christoph. Buondelmonti, Florentini, Librum insularum archipelagi e Codicibus Parisinus regiis nunc primum totum edidit*, and published in Leipzig and Berlin, in 1824. It should be noted that von Sinner conflates two different versions of Buondelmonti's manuscript though without making this clear (Turner, "Christopher Buondelmonti," p. 13). Courtesy of The University of Chicago Library, Special Collections Research Center. The accompanying image of Constantinople (fig. 39) is attributed to Pietro del Massaio (fl. 1455–1475) and is based on Buondelmonti's earlier view. It is reproduced from one of three fifteenth-century manuscript Ptolemy atlases that contain city views, Paris BN Lat. 4802, with permission of the Bibliothèque Nationale, Paris.

Bernhard von Breydenbach, ca. 1440–1497   Figures 41 & 47
[*Peregrinatio in Terram Sanctam*]. Speier: Peter Drach, 29 July 1490

The first edition of the *Peregrinatio* was printed in Mainz by Erhard Reuwich, the artist who accompanied Breydenbach, in 1486. Although Breydenbach is described as the author, the original text appears to have been prepared by Martin Roth. It was followed by two further editions printed in Mainz between 1486 and 1488, and a French edition printed in Lyons in 1489. The maps and city views in all these editions, as well as the 1490 edition printed in Speier, on exhibit, and a later, 1498, edition printed in Zaragoza, are printed from the same woodblocks, which must therefore have traveled a considerable distance across Europe despite their fragility (Campbell, *Earliest Printed Maps*, pp. 93–94). The University of Chicago Library, Special Collections Research Center.

Giovanni Battista Ramusio, 1495–1557   Figures 8 & 23
Delle Navigationi et Viaggi, Raccolto da M. Gio. Batt. Ramvsio & con molti vaghi discorsi .... Primo volume & Terza editione. Venice: Stamperia de Givnti, 1563

The three volumes of Ramusio's *Delle Navigationi et Viaggi* appeared in print between 1550 and 1559 (the first edition of Volume 1 was published in 1550, followed by Volume 3 in 1556, and Volume 2 in 1559). The volume included in the exhibit is the third edition of Volume 1, printed in 1563, which includes additional narratives and three maps attributed to Gastaldi. Ramusio had completed work on Volume 2 shortly before his death in 1557, but a disastrous fire destroyed the woodblocks for both the text and maps and delayed publication until 1559. It was not until a 1563 edition of Volume 1 that Ramusio's role as compiler and editor was fully acknowledged in the title and a tribute added to the foreword by the publisher (Parks, "Contents and Sources," p. 294). Courtesy of The University of Chicago Library, Special Collections Research Center.

Nicolas de Nicolay, 1517–1583   Figures 44 & 45
Le Navigationi et Viaggi, fatti nella Turchia …. Venice: Francesco Ziletti, 1580

The first edition of Nicolay's account of his journey to Istanbul was published as *Les qvatre premiers livres des navigations et peregrinations orientales, de N. de Nicolay* in 1567, although most copies have a title page dated 1568 (Karrow, *Mapmakers*, p. 440). The next edition, published in Antwerp in 1576, appeared under the title *Les navigations, peregrinations et voyages, faicts en le Tvriqvie, par Nicolas de Nicolay Daulphinoys, seigneur d'Arfeville.* The copy on display in the exhibit is an Italian edition published in Venice in 1580, which includes seven plates not found in the original edition. The O. J. Sopranos Collection.

Jean-Baptiste Tavernier, 1605–1689   Not Illustrated
Les six voyages de Jean Baptiste Tavernier, Ecuyer Baron D'Aubonne, qu'il a fait en Turquie, en Perse, et aux Indes …. Paris: Gervais Clouzier …, 1677

Tavernier's account of his six "voyages" to Turkey, Persia, and India, between 1631 and 1668, was among the most popular of French travel narratives, being reprinted over twenty times before the mid-eighteenth century, along with English, Dutch, Italian, and German translations. The first edition, included in the exhibit, was expanded in later printings to include additional material. Courtesy of The University of Chicago Library, Special Collections Research Center.

Laurent d'Arvieux, Chevalier, 1635–1702   Figure 24
Voyage fait par ordre du Roy Louis XIV dans le Palestine, vers le Grand Emir, Chef des Princes Arabes du Desert …. Par D. L. R. *[de la Roque].* Paris: Chez André Gailleau, M.DCC.XVII [1717]

D'Arvieux's major claim to fame was a treaty he negotiated with Tunisia in 1668 to free Frenchmen then being held in captivity. He later served as French ambassador in Istanbul and as consul in Algiers. This edition includes as an appendix the first French translation (by Jean de la Roque) of Abu al-Fida's description of the geography of the Arabian peninsula, including tables of the latitude and longitude of towns that Abu al-Fida had compiled using Ptolemy's calculations. Courtesy of The University of Chicago Library, Special Collections Research Center.

Cornelis de Bruijn, 1652–ca. 1726   Figure 48
Reizen van Cornelis de Bruyn, door de Vermaardtse Deelen van Klein Asie ….
Delft: Henrik van Krooneveld, 1698

This first edition of de Bruijn's account of his travels through the Ottoman empire between 1677 and 1684 is profusely illustrated with engravings made from his own drawings and sketches. A French translation, *Voyage au Levant …,* was published in 1700, and an English edition, *A Voyage to the Levant: Or, Travels in the Principal Parts of Asia Minor, the Islands of Scio, Rhodes, Cyprus, & with an Account of the most Considerable Cities of Egypt, Syria and the Holy Land,* appeared in 1702. The O. J. Sopranos Collection.

Jean de la Roque, 1661–ca. 1743   Not Illustrated
Voyage de l'Arabie heureuse ..., fait par les françois pour la premiere fois, dans les années 1708, 1709 & 1710 ...;
avec ... un memoire concernant l'arbre & le fruit du café .... Paris: Chez André Gailleau ..., MDCCXVI [1716]

Jean de la Roque's edited account of the experiences of French merchants from St. Malo who traveled to Mocha in
the early eighteenth century seeking direct access to the coffee trade, together with his own memoir on coffee, was
published in Paris in 1716. His account aroused considerable interest, and English translations appeared in 1726,
1732, and 1742. Courtesy of The University of Chicago Library, Special Collections Research Center.

Lady Mary Wortley Montagu, 1689–1762   Not Illustrated
Letters of the Right Honourable Lady M—y W—y M—e, Written During Her Travels in Europe, Asia, and Africa,
to Persons of Distinction, Men of Letters, &c in Different Parts of Europe .... London, Printed for A. Holmes ...,
MDCCLXIV [1764]

Lady Mary Montagu's *Embassy Letters*, written during her stay in Istanbul, appeared in print for the first time in
1763, shortly after her death. The letters in this unauthorized edition were quickly pirated, and the editors of the
edition included in the exhibit appended a series of additional letters that they alleged had been written by Lady
Mary. These spurious letters were themselves reprinted by other editors (Grundy, *Lady Mary*). Courtesy of The
University of Chicago Library, Special Collections Research Center.

Carsten Niebuhr, 1733–1815   Figures 49 & 50
Description de l'Arabie, d'aprés les observations et recherches faites dans le pays meme. Par M. Niebuhr,
Capitaine d'Ingenieurs, Membre de la Société Royale de Gottingen. Nouvelle édition. Paris: Chez Brunet,
M.DCC.LXXIX [1779]

Following his return to Denmark in 1767 with a huge collection of manuscripts, specimens, observations, and
sketches, Niebuhr spent several years cataloguing and analyzing the expedition's findings. The first report summa-
rizing the results and describing the difficulties that the expedition had confronted, *Beschreibung von Arabien ...*, was
published in Copenhagen in 1772. Courtesy of The University of Chicago Library, Special Collections Research
Center.

M. G. F. A. Comte de Choiseul-Gouffier, 1752–1817   Figures 43 & 52
Voyage pittoresque de la Grece, Volume 1. Paris: J. J. Blaise, 1782

The first volume of Choiseul-Gouffier's *Voyage pittoresque de la Grece* was first published in Paris in 1782, prior to his
appointment as the French ambassador to the Ottoman Porte. The book included engravings based on the sketches
and drawings of French artists and architects who had visited Greece and the Aegean islands under the patronage of
the Marquis de Chabart. The text of the first volume was considerably revised in later editions to remove much of
Choiseul-Gouffier's views on Ottoman suppression of Greek liberty. Choiseul-Gouffier spent the later years of the
French Revolution in exile and completed the second volume of *Voyage pittoresque* only after his return to France,
when he became a Minister of State following the restoration of the monarchy. The O. J. Sopranos Collection.

M. Constantin-François Volney, 1757–1820   Not Illustrated

Voyage en Syrie et en Égypte: pendant les années 1783, 1784 et 1785 … avec deux cartes géographiques.
Nouvelle édition. Paris: 1792

The first edition of *Voyage en Syrie et en Égypte* was published in 1787; Volney's *Considérations sur la guerre actuelle des Turcs* was published in Paris in 1788. From Napoleon's memoirs, we know that Volney's works were consulted in planning the French expedition to Egypt in 1798. Volney had speculated on the possibility of French administration of Egypt and the Levant as a way of achieving necessary "scientific improvements" in the administration of the region. Although he ultimately concluded that such a project was impractical, such speculation reflected the changing power relations between the Ottoman empire and the dominant European powers of the late eighteenth century, France and Britain. Courtesy of The University of Chicago Library, Special Collections Research Center.

ENDNOTES

EUROPEAN CARTOGRAPHERS AND THE OTTOMAN WORLD

[1] It is generally accepted that Oronce Fine was the first to use the cordiform ("heart-shaped") projection for a 1519 manuscript world map dedicated to François I, King of France. However, the principles of such a projection had been outlined by earlier mathematicians, including Johannes Werner, who illustrated it in print. Fine's 1519 map has not survived and is only known through a reference to such an undertaking in the preface to Fine's later printed world map (also using a cordiform projection), dating from 1534. The oldest extant world map using the cosmographic heart projection was published by the German mathematician and cosmographer Peter Apian, in 1530 (Kish, "Cosmographic Heart"). It has been argued that Apian worked from Fine's earlier manuscript map, but as Karrow (*Mapmakers*, p. 171) has noted, the geography is quite different and he could equally well have worked independently from Werner's drawing.

[2] The first volume of Ramusio's *Delle Navigationi et Viaggi* (1550) opens with a history of Africa written by al-Hasan ibn Muhammad al-Fasi. Born in the city of Granada in the late fifteenth century, when the city was still under Muslim rule, al-Hasan ibn Muhammad had traveled extensively in Africa before being captured by corsairs while returning to Tunis from Egypt. He was presented as a slave to Pope Leo X, who baptized him and gave him the name Leo Africanus (Parks, "Contents and Sources," p. 282). According to Ramusio's preface, Leo translated his history into Italian around the year 1526. Leo Africanus is believed to have escaped or been released from captivity, returning to Africa, where he died ca. 1550. The similarities between the experience of Leo Africanus and the story attributed to Hajji Ahmed by the author of the "Turkish" map are quite striking.

[3] Ménage suggests that, in pursuing this market, Giustinian sought an individual who could help him prepare a text that would appeal to his intended audience. However, he ended up with someone who, although familiar with the language of the Ottoman chancery, "had an imperfect knowledge of both Arabic and Turkish, and a good but not intimate knowledge of the Moslem world and Moslem habits of thought, someone who was acquainted with Ramusio's *Viaggi* and through it knew of 'Sultan Ismael [Abu al-Fida]'" (Ménage, "Map of Hajji Ahmed," p. 311). The individual who best fits this description appears to be the [Michele] Membré mentioned in the license who was an associate of Ramusio's and the official Turkish translator for the Venetian Republic.

[4] No copies of the map survive from the sixteenth century. Although Giustinian was released, the woodblocks remained in the Venetian archives and were apparently forgotten until 1795, when twenty-four impressions were made by the official printer for Simone Assemani, a professor of oriental languages at the University of Padua (Karrow, *Mapmakers*, p. 172).

[5] Mangani ("Abraham Ortelius") provides a further intriguing glimpse into these cultural and textual exchanges, suggesting that the French oriental scholar and linguist Guillaume Postel could have played a role in the Hajji Ahmed map as a way of encouraging contacts between "west" and "east." Postel was almost certainly an acquaintance of Oronce Fine's in Paris, where they both taught mathematics, and it seems likely that Fine's cordiform projection with its intellectual and moral ideas would have strongly appealed to Postel's vision of a universal religion and a universal state as a symbol of the unity of human thought. Moreover, it was Postel who introduced Abu al-Fida's geography to Ramusio. (For further discussion of Postel's connections with Venetian humanist scholars and cartographers, see the essay *Abu al-Fida* [pp. 53–55].) "If he had had a hand in the production of a map expressly designed for [Süleyman's] court, the move would have been typical of his constant promotion of his doctrine of *concordia mundi*, a two-way process designed to bring Christian material to the attention of Arabs, Turks, and Hebrews while at the same time translating the most important eastern texts for use in the west" (Mangani, "Abraham Ortelius," p. 68).

[6] The possibility that one of these commissions may have been the original model for the Hajji Ahmed map has been raised by several authors (see, for example, Fabris, "Note sul mappamondo"). However, Arbel ("Maps of the

World") makes a compelling argument against such a connection based on descriptions and measurements of the maps authorized in the licenses. For a close reasoning of ways in which Giustinian may have acquired the map and then sought to regularize his position under the Venetian law of privilege, see Arbel, "Maps of the World," pp. 24–26.

[7] What happened to Ptolemy's work between its completion in the second century A.D. and the transmission of the first manuscript copies from Constantinople to Italy early in the fifteenth century has been the subject of endless scholarly debate. The dominant view is that the maps (the earliest extant manuscript maps date from the thirteenth century) are the product of later Arab and Byzantine scholarship.

[8] As many scholars have pointed out, much more was involved than the simple transmission of Ptolemy's ideas and maps. The newfound ability to repeatedly reproduce the same image helped create a standardized visual image of the world and its regions and a common cartographic vocabulary for mapmakers and readers alike, something that had been unimaginable with unique and highly individualistic manuscripts, no matter how gifted a copyist might be (see, for example, Brotton, *Trading Territories*, pp. 35–37).

[9] Campbell (*Earliest Printed Maps*, pp. 5–7) has argued that such was the influence and authority of Ptolemy's text that maps of the late fifteenth century actually display less knowledge of Asia than the earlier medieval *Catalan Atlas* of 1375 and Fra Mauro's world map of 1459, which include information brought back by Marco Polo.

[10] As Campbell (*Earliest Printed Maps*, p. 124) has pointed out, it is not, strictly speaking, correct to describe Berlinghieri's text as an edition of Ptolemy; rather it is a description of the world in Italian verse derived from classical and contemporary sources that seems to have been in preparation as early as 1464. Perhaps more than any other edition, Berlinghieri's text expresses the Ptolemaic perspective on the globe as an intellectual vision "demonstrating how with true discipline, we can leap within ourselves, without the aid of wings, so that we may view the earth through an image marked on a parchment" (quoted in Cosgrove, *Apollo's Eye*, p. 109).

[11] The Venetian Council of Ten referred to Gastaldi as "Master Giacomo Piemontese, our cosmographer"; the honorific "cosmographer to the Republic of Venice" comes from Vincenzo Coronelli, who was himself officially appointed to that position in the late seventeenth century (Karrow, *Mapmakers*, p. 216).

[12] The commissioning of large mural maps showing the latest geographical discoveries as wall decorations was quite common in the late fifteenth and sixteenth centuries. As Schulz ("Maps as Metaphores") has noted, through their ornamentation and content these maps often conveyed a wide range of political and ideological intentions, while also serving to enhance the power and learning of the patron in a very public setting. Gastaldi's first commission, in 1549, was for a map of Africa showing the latest discoveries to decorate the wall of the Sala dello Scudo, the room used to display the heraldic shields of the Doge of Venice. A second commission followed in 1553, when Gastaldi was asked to prepare a design for a map to be painted on the wall of the Sala della Mappa that would show "all the relations given by the captains ... Alvaro Nunez, Jacques Cartier the Frenchman for New France, Joan de Barros for the geography of China, and the book of the messer Marco Polo for Cathay" (Karrow, *Mapmakers*, pp. 224, 226).

[13] I am very grateful to Robert Karrow, Map Curator at The Newberry Library, for his help in making sense of the licensing and publication history of Gastaldi's maps. For example, Fabris ("Note sul mappamondo") refers to a privilege granted to Gastaldi in March 1559 by the inquisitor-general in Venice (Felice Peretti, later Pope Sixtus V) for publication of a work entitled *Cosmografia della Natolia e del viaggio da Venezia a Costantinopoli*. However, no map by that exact title is known to exist, although Karrow notes that Gastaldi's map of southeastern Europe, from Venice at its far left edge to Istanbul at the far right edge, separately licensed and printed in Venice in 1559, fits this description very closely. The privilege for this map of southeastern Europe was issued the same day as the privilege for the three-part map of Asia included in the exhibit (fig. 7) (Karrow, personal communication).

[14] The first volume of *Delle Navigationi et Viaggi* was published in 1550 and included travel accounts of Africa, India, and the East Indies. It included only a single woodcut map of the Nile. Later editions of the first volume included additional narratives and, beginning in 1554, three maps of the East Indies, India, and Africa. Ramusio had completed work on the second volume, covering the rest of Asia including Persia, Syria, the Arabian peninsula, and Anatolia, shortly before his death in 1557. However, a disastrous fire in the printer's workshop later that year destroyed both the type and the woodblocks for the accompanying maps. Publication of this volume, in which the

travels of Marco Polo take pride of place, did not occur until 1559. The third volume, which was concerned with accounts of the Americas, appeared in 1556 (Parks, "Contents and Sources").

[15] Tibbetts' analysis of the nomenclature on Gastaldi's earlier maps of the Arabian peninsula (including the *Arabia Felix nova tabvla* that he prepared for the 1548 Venetian edition of Ptolemy) suggests that Gastaldi was not familiar with the travel narrative of Ludovico di Varthema of Bologna, who had traveled through the Hejaz and visited the interior of Yemen en route to India in the early sixteenth century, until it was made available to him by Ramusio. This account appears in Ramusio's collection and, beginning with the 1561 map of Asia, Gastaldi's mapping of the Arabian peninsula incorporates information from Varthema.

[16] Goodrich ("Ottoman Americana") has identified four accounts of the New World by five authors that provide the source material for the *Tarih-i Hindi-i Garbi*. Goodrich concludes, on the basis of the internal spelling and grammar of the manuscript, that its author was working either from Italian editions or translations of these works. In two cases these accounts were also reproduced in the third volume of Ramusio's *Delle Navigationi et Viaggi*, published in 1556. That the Ottoman copyists were familiar with the *Navigationi et Viaggi* is clear from a fairly complete translation of its table of contents, inscribed in a ca. 1600 copy of *Tarih-i Hindi-i Garbi* in the Topkapı Palace Library (Goodrich, "Ottoman Americana," n. 44).

[17] The earliest surviving copy of this manuscript is from the late sixteenth century and was a presentation copy produced for Sultan Murad III. However, Goodrich ("Ottoman Americana") concludes that the copy from The Newberry Library (ca. 1600) displayed in the exhibit is closest to the original. There are more than twenty known manuscript copies of the text from the seventeenth century, including one that is a translation of the text into Persian (Goodrich, "*Tarih-i Hindi-i Garbi*").

[18] Some of the ideas in this section of the essay were initially presented in a paper, "Mapping the Ottoman World: Alternative Cartographies and the Visualization of Political Space," jointly authored with Kay Ebel, at a conference on Middle Eastern Geography in the Twenty-First Century at The University of Texas at Austin, April 4–5, 2003.

[19] Although Sanson died in 1677, his maps (and also his reputation) continued to be promoted by his heirs (Pastoureau, *Les Sansons*). Shortly after Sanson's death, his son Guillaume entered into a new publishing arrangement with Alexis-Hubert Jaillot (1632–1712), and many of Sanson's maps were re-engraved for inclusion in the *Atlas Nouveau* published under the patronage of the Dauphin in 1681. Jaillot's maps and world atlases, finely engraved, richly decorated, and printed on high-quality paper, were celebrations of the French monarchy and intended to appeal to the wealthy and privileged. After the death of Sanson's grandson, the task of maintaining Sanson's reputation as "le prince des géographes de son temps" passed to Gilles Robert de Vaugondy (1688–1766), who inherited Sanson's notes and sketches, using them in conjunction with materials acquired from Jaillot to publish world atlases, first under his own name and later in collaboration with his son, Didier (1726–1786).

[20] Lach (*Asia*, pp. 314–31) has pointed particularly to the role of Jesuit missionaries in adding significantly to European knowledge of Asia from the sixteenth century onwards through their letters and published reports, which were widely disseminated. Both Sanson and d'Anville benefited from their close association with the Society of Jesus. Sanson was educated at a Jesuit school in Amiens at a time when the Jesuits were extremely active in educational reform in France. Pastoureau ("French School Atlases") sees clear evidence of this training in Sanson's approach to mapping and in the strongly didactic quality of his maps and geographical tables. D'Anville's notable contribution to the improved mapping of Asia drew heavily from surveys and source materials sent to him by Jesuit missionaries.

[21] The phrase is taken from Larry Wolff's translation of a passage from Robert de Vaugondy's *Atlas Universal* of 1725 (Wolff, *Inventing Eastern Europe*, p. 148).

[22] The complex history of Ottoman relationships with neighboring European states in the eighteenth and nineteenth centuries is well beyond the scope of this book. However, the Treaty of Karlowitz (1699), which followed a disastrous series of Ottoman defeats and losses in the aftermath of the failed Siege of Vienna in 1683, may be said to mark a new phase in Ottoman history (Quataert, *Ottoman Empire*). "For the first time, an Ottoman sovereign formally acknowledged his defeat and the permanent loss of (rather than temporarily withdrawal from) lands conquered by his ancestors" (ibid., p. 38). Quataert characterizes the dispiriting eighteenth-century Ottoman military experience as "wars of contraction" and the reasons for the series of defeats and territorial losses have been end-

lessly discussed and debated by historians. However, as Quataert observes, it is important to recognize that the era was not one of unrelenting retreat and accelerating decline since there were periodic successes both military and diplomatic. Moreover, Ottoman diplomats were often able to take advantage of European rivalries to retain territories that might otherwise have been lost. For an excellent discussion of this period and the important political and social transformations that were taking place simultaneously in the Ottoman state, see Quataert, *Ottoman Empire*.

[23] The career of Luigi Ferdinando, Comte de Marsigli (1658–1730), exemplifies the peripatetic, "nationless," soldier-engineer-scientist who were to be found seeking employment and advancement in courts and chanceries across Europe in the sixteenth and seventeenth centuries. Born into a well-established family in Bologna and educated accordingly, he found employment in the service of the Republic of Venice and accompanied the Venetian ambassador to Istanbul in 1679. While in Istanbul he seems to have moved easily among a handful of scholars and intellectuals close to the court, including Ebu Bekir ibn Behram el-Dimaşki, who had been officially commissioned to translate a copy of Blaeu's world atlas. Marsigli's diary records that Ebu Bekir had told him that there was a great deal of misinformation as well as fact in Blaeu's coverage of the sultan's domains (Stoye, *Marsigli's Europe*, p. 25). Later, Marsigli took service in the Habsburg army, was taken prisoner, and spent the Siege of Vienna (1683) digging ditches and brewing coffee for the Ottoman besiegers. Briefly imprisoned in Bosnia, he escaped and, returning to the Habsburg army, spent the next decade on a variety of assignments surveying the Austrian/Hungarian/Ottoman borderlands. Throughout his career he was an enthusiastic naturalist and pursued a range of scientific hobbies that included measuring the flow of rivers, sketching plants, and collecting fossils. After his years in France, he returned to Bologna, where he set up an Institute of Sciences and Arts to house his specimens, models, and sketches, and established a printing house. For an excellent biography, see Stoye, *Marsigli's Europe*.

THE MEDITERRANEAN TRADITION OF CHARTING

[24] The earliest extant portolan charts date from the late twelfth century. The term is derived from the Italian word *portolano*, a compilation in written form of sailing directions — including lists of places, distances, compass bearings, and coastal hazards — useful to mariners. At some stage, these were presumably transcribed into graphic form, and hence the term portolan chart implicitly suggests that the maps supplemented the written account (Campbell, "Portolan Charts," p. 375).

[25] The text of Berlinghieri's description of the world in his 1482 edition of Ptolemy, for example, makes reference to a portolan chart of the Mediterranean, although the maps produced to accompany the text appear to be based on different sources (Campbell, *Earliest Printed Maps*, p. 124). Other editors of Ptolemy, such as Bernardus Sylvanus, clearly made use of portolan charts in seeking to update the regional maps. Cosgrove (*Apollo's Eye*, p. 90) notes that, following Martin Waldseemüller's prototype *carta marina* of 1516, sixteenth-century editions of the *Geographia* acknowledged the distinctive perspective of the navigator, regularly incorporating alongside the Ptolemaic maps hydrographic world maps modeled on the portolan chart with cardinal points, compass roses, and rhumb lines.

[26] For an excellent review of these arguments, see Campbell ("Portolan Charts"), who makes a compelling case that the appearance of the portolan chart is linked in some way with other improvements in navigation, particularly the mariner's compass (in use in the Mediterranean early in the thirteenth century) and compass card divided into sixteen points or multiples thereof. But whether the compass card imitated or inspired the system represented on the charts is unclear.

[27] For a discussion of the development and spread of this lingua franca and the assortment of linguistic and nautical terms associated with it, see Kahane and Tietze, *Lingua Franca*.

[28] Particularly prominent in the field of publishing printed sea charts was Willem Blaeu, whose pre-eminence was recognized by his appointment as hydrographer to the Dutch East India Company, in which post he was succeeded by his son, Joan. In addition to collating information received from Dutch navigators and providing updated charts, the hydrographer edited and printed charts for commercial sale. This was very different from the practice in Lisbon and Seville, where every effort was made to keep knowledge of new discoveries and navigational charts within the control of the state.

[29] Although published first (in 1595), the *Reysgheschrift vande navigation der Portualoyses in Orienten* forms the second part of the complete text, which appeared in 1596 under the title *Itinerario, voyage ofte schipvaert van Jan Huygen van Linschoten naar Oost-ofte Portugalis Indien*. The first part of the text is the itinerary proper, which includes descriptions of the coastlines of Africa and the Americas, written with the assistance of Bernardus Paludanus. Paludanus also collaborated with Linschoten on the third section, the *Beschryving*, which was a general survey of the geography and natural history of the new discoveries compiled from published sources.

THROUGH THE EYES OF TRAVELERS

[30] There is an extensive literature discussing the ideas, observations, and narratives of pre-modern European travelers to the "Orient." Among the more recent studies that are particularly helpful in re-assessing the literary output of travelers in the Ottoman empire are: Brandon H. Beck, *From the Rising of the Sun: English Images of the Ottoman Empire to 1715* (New York: Peter Lang, 1987); Glen J. Ames and Ronald S. Love (eds.), *Distant Lands and Diverse Cultures: The French Experience in Asia, 1600–1700* (Westport, Connecticut and London: Praeger, 2003); Gerald MacLean, *The Rise of Oriental Travel: English Visitors to the Ottoman Empire, 1580–1720* (Basingstoke, England and New York: Palgrave, 2004); Gerald MacLean (ed.), *Re-Orienting the Renaissance: Cultural Exchanges with the East* (Basingstoke, England and New York: Palgrave Macmillan, 2005); and Rhoads Murphey, "Bigots or Informed Observers? A Periodization of Pre-Colonial English and European Writing on the Middle East," *Journal of the American Oriental Society* 110 (1990): 291–303. The most comprehensive account of travelers in the Ottoman empire is Stephane Yerasimos, *Les voyageurs dans l'empire Ottoman (XIVᵉ–XVIᵉ siècles)* (Ankara: Imprimeries de la Société Turque d'Histoire, 1991).

[31] This idea is particularly well explored in the wider context of European knowledge of Asia in Donald Lach's seminal study, *Asia in the Making of Europe*.

[32] At some stage during his travels in India, Tavernier acquired a large uncut stone which he later sold to Louis XIV. This became known as the "French Blue" diamond, which disappeared at the time of the French Revolution; it is generally accepted that the "Hope" diamond, now housed in the Smithsonian Institution, was cut from this larger stone.

[33] Letter dated 17 June 1717 to Lady [   ], identified by some editors as Lady Rich. Lady Mary had herself been badly scarred by smallpox and while in Istanbul became interested in the Turkish practice of inoculation (variolation) against the illness. She had her son inoculated, and on return to England became a courageous and fierce advocate of the practice, despite widespread opposition and ridicule from the medical community (Grundy, *Lady Mary*).

CARTOGRAPHY AND GEOGRAPHICAL CONSCIOUSNESS IN THE OTTOMAN EMPIRE (1453-1730)

[34] For the purposes of this essay, the period between 1453 and 1730 are considered as the "early modern" period.

[35] Mehmed II is known to have used the title Kayzer-i Rum (Roman Caesar) in his correspondences with the European rulers.

[36] For the construction and resettlement policies of Mehmed II and their role in the formation of the imperial enterprise, see İnalcık, "Ottoman State"; Necipoğlu, *Architecture*, pp. xii-xx, 3-22; Yerasimos, "Osmanlı İstanbul'unun Kuruluşu"; and Kafesçioğlu, "Ottoman Capital."

[37] It is not clear in the literature whether Amirutzes of Trebizond and George of Trebizond from Crete were the same person or not (Necipoğlu, *Architecture*, p. 12).

[38] Francesco Berlinghieri, *Atlas*, TKS G. I. 84. Cited in K. Pinto, "Ways of Seeing," p. 11.

[39] Paolo Santini da Duccio, *Tractus de re militari et machinis bellicis*, Bibliothèque Nationale, Paris (Cod. Lat. 7239).

[40] Al-Istakhri, *Kitab al-Masalik wa al-Mamalik*, TKS Ahmed 2830.

[41] Piri Re'is, *World Map* (1513), TKS Revan Köşkü 1633 mük. This map was published in Afetinan, *Piri Reis'in Hayatı*.

[42] Piri Re'is, *Kitab-ı Bahriye*, Süleymaniye Ayasofya 2612. Today there are forty-five manuscript copies of this second version in libraries around the world (Özen, Piri Reis, pp. 17, 20–22). There are 5,658 manuscript maps in the forty-two known copies of the work. Nine of these copies are located in libraries in England, Italy, France, Germany, and Australia. The rest are listed in the catalogues of different libraries and museums in Istanbul. Among the forty-five manuscripts of the work, two of them include only text; three consist exclusively of maps.

[43] Piri Re'is, *Kitab-ı Bahriye*, Süleymaniye Ayasofya 2612. This copy in the Süleymaniye Library is attested to be the most complete copy. It was donated to the library by Mahmud I (r. 1730–1754).

[44] This paragraph is based on Liu, "Comparative and Critical Study"; Kahle "Islamische Quelle"; Schefer, "Trois chapitres"; and Zenker, "Chinesische Reich."

[45] Ali Ekber Hitayi, *Khitay-nameh*, Süleymaniye Re'isü'l-küttab 609 mük. (Translations to Ottoman Turkish: Süleymaniye Ayasofya 3188, TKS Esad Efendi 1852.). 46 Ali Ekber Hitayi, Khitay-nameh, Süleymaniye Ayasofiya 3188; TKS Esad Efendi 1852; Dresdener Bibliothek, Morgenlandische Handschriften, Nr. 71; Berlin Bibliothek, Hs. Diez A. 8°. oct. 95 and Hs. or. Qu. 898.

[46] *Tarih-i Hind-i Garbi*, TKS Revan Köşkü 1488.

[47] *Tarih-i Hind-i Garbi*, Ayer MS 612, The Newberry Library, Chicago.

[48] Ali Macar Re'is, *Atlas*, TKS Hazine 644.

[49] Also, the Black Sea was the hinterland of Istanbul and in the sixteenth century there was a constant commercial traffic between the major ports of the northern Black Sea and Istanbul. This alone might be a good reason why these atlases open with the Black Sea chart (İnalcık, "Ottoman State").

[50] According to Mirco Vedovato, "the chart is a copy of an original work by an Italian cartographer commissioned by Mohammed Raus, who, as appears from his title, may be considered the captain of some ship of the Turkish Navy" (Vedovato, "Nautical Chart"). On the chart of Mehmed Re'is, see also Brice, Imber, and Lorch, *Aegean Sea-Chart*.

[51] Anonymous, *Ottoman Portolan Chart*. Bayerische Staatsbibliothek (Handschriften Abteilung), Cod. turc. 431.

[52] The Süleymaniye Library holds three more copies of the same work: Katib Çelebi, *Levami'u'n-Nur fi Zulmeti Atlas Minor*, Süleymaniye 988; Süleymaniye 2042; Köprülü Ahmed Paşa 178.

BIBLIOGRAPHY

Abou-el-Haj, Rifaat. "The Formal Closure of the Ottoman Frontier in Europe, 1699-1703." *Journal of the American Oriental Society* 89 (1969): 467-75.

Adıvar, Adnan. *Osmanlı Türklerinde İlim*. 4th edition. Istanbul: Remzi Kitabevi, 1991.

Afetinan, Ayşe. *Piri Reis'in Hayatı ve Eserleri: Amerika'nın En Eski Haritaları*. 2nd edition. Ankara: TTK, 1987.

Akerman, James R. "The Structuring of Political Territory in Early Printed Atlases." *Imago Mundi* 47 (1995): 138-54.

Ames, Glenn J., and Ronald S. Love, editors. *Distant Lands and Diverse Cultures: The French Experience in Asia, 1600-1700*. Westport, CT: Praeger, 2003.

d'Anville, Jean Baptiste Bourguignon. *L'Empire Turc considéré dans son établissement et dans ses accroissements successifs*. Paris: De l'Imprimerie royale, 1772.

Arbel, Benjamin. "Maps of the World for Ottoman Princes? Further Evidence and Questions Concerning 'The Mappamondo of Hajji Ahmed.'" *Imago Mundi* 54 (2002): 19-29.

Babinger, Franz. "An Italian Map of the Balkans, Presumably Owned by Mehmed II, The Conqueror (1452-53)." *Imago Mundi* 8 (1951): 8-15.

——. *Mehmed the Conqueror and His Time*. Translated by R. Manheim, edited by W. C. Hickman. Bollingen Series 96. Princeton: Princeton University Press, 1978.

Bagrow, Leo. *History of Cartography*. Revised and enlarged by R. A. Skelton. Cambridge, MA: Harvard University Press, 1964.

Berger, Albrecht, and Jonathan Bardill. "The Representation of Constantinople in Hartmann Schedel's *World Chronicle*, and Related Pictures." *Byzantine and Modern Greek Studies* 22 (1998): 2-37.

Berkes, Niyazi. "Ibrāhīm Müteferriḳa." *Encyclopaedia of Islam*, edited by: P. Bearman, Th. Bianquis, C. E. Bosworth, E. van Donzel, and W. P. Heinrichs. Brill, 2007. *Brill Online*. University of Chicago Libraries. 27 August 2007. http://www.brillonline.nl.proxy.uchicago.edu/subscriber/entry?entry=islam_SIM-3456.

Bostan, İdris. "Cezayir-i Bahrı Sefid Eyaleti'nin Kuruluşu (1534)." *İstanbul Üniversitesi Edebiyat Fakültesi Tarih Dergisi* 38 (2002-2003): 61-77.

Boyer, M. Christine. *The City of Collective Memory: Its Historical Imagery and Architectural Entertainments*. Cambridge, MA: M.I.T. Press, 1994.

[Braun, Georg, and Frans Hogenberg]. *Civitates Orbis Terrarum*. Book III: *Urbium praecipvarum totius mundi liber tertius*. [Cologne], 1581.

Brice, William C., and Colin H. Imber. "Turkish Charts in the 'Portolan' Style." *Geographical Journal* 144 (1978): 528-29.

Brice, William C.; Colin H. Imber; and Richard Lorch. *The Aegean Sea-Chart of Mehmed Reis Ibn Menemenli, A.D. 1590/1*. Manchester: University of Manchester Press, 1977.

van den Broecke, Marcel P. R. *Ortelius Atlas Maps: An Illustrated Guide*. Netherlands: HES Publishers, 1996.

Brotton, Jerry. *Trading Territories: Mapping the Early Modern World*. New York: Cornell University Press, 1998.

Brown, Lloyd A. *The Story of Maps*. Boston: Little, Brown, 1949.

Brummett, Palmira. "The Overrated Adversary: Rhodes and Ottoman Naval Power." *The Historical Journal* 36 (1993): 517-41.

Buisseret, David. "Monarchs, Ministers and Maps in France before the Accession of Louis XIV." In *Monarchs, Ministers and Maps: The Emergence of Cartography as a Tool of Government in Early Modern Europe*, edited by David Buisseret, pp. 99–124. Chicago: University of Chicago Press, 1992.

Campbell, Tony. *The Earliest Printed Maps, 1472–1500*. Berkeley and Los Angeles: University of California Press, 1987.

——. "Portolan Charts from the Late Thirteenth Century to 1500." In *The History of Cartography*, Vol. 1, edited by J. B. Harley and D. Woodward, pp. 371–463. Chicago: University of Chicago Press, 1987.

Casale, Giancarlo. "The Ottoman Age of Exploration: Spices Maps and Conquests in the Sixteenth Century Ottoman Empire." Ph.D. diss., Harvard University, 2004.

Codazzi, A. "Una descrizione del Cairo di Guglielmo Postel." In *Studi in onore di Cesare Maneresi*, pp. 169–206. Milan, 1952.

Cosgrove, Denis. *Apollo's Eye: A Cartographic Genealogy of the Earth in the Western Imagination*. Baltimore and London: Johns Hopkins University Press, 2001.

——. "Contested Global Visions: *One World, Whole Earth*, and the Apollo Space Photographs." *Annals of the Association of American Geographers* 84 (1994): 270–94.

Dankoff, Robert. "The Intimate Life of an Ottoman Statesman: Melek Ahmed Pasha (1588–1662)." In *Evliya Çelebi's Book of Travels* (Seyahat-name). New York: State University of New York Press, 1991.

Dannenfeldt, Karl H. *Leonhard Rauwolf: Sixteenth-Century Physician, Botanist, and Traveler*. Cambridge, MA: Harvard University Press, 1968.

Davies, Hugh Wm. *Bernhard von Breydenbach and his Journey to the Holy Land, 1483–1484*. London: J. & J. Leighton, 1911.

Destombes, Marcel. "Guillaume Postel cartographe." In *Guillaume Postel, 1581–1981; Colloque International d'Avranches*, pp. 361–71. Paris: Éditions de la Maisnie, 1985.

Ebel, Kathryn Ann. "City Views, Imperial Visions: Cartography and the Visual Culture of Urban Space in the Ottoman Empire, 1453–1603." Ph.D. dissertation, Department of Geography, The University of Texas at Austin, 2002.

Edgerton, Samuel Y., Jr. "From Mental Matrix to *Mappamundi* to Christian Empire: The Heritage of Ptolemaic Cartography in the Renaissance." In *Art and Cartography: Six Historical Essays*, edited by David Woodward, pp. 10–50. The Kenneth Nebenzahl, Jr., Lectures in the History of Cartography. Chicago: University of Chicago Press, 1987.

——. *The Renaissance Rediscovery of Linear Perspective*. New York: Basic Books, 1975.

Fabris, Antonio. "Note sul mappamondo cordiforme di Haci Ahmed di Tunisi." *Quaderni di studi Arabi* 7 (1989): 3–17.

Faroqhi, Suraiya. *The Ottoman Empire and the World Around It*. London and New York: I. B. Tauris, 2004.

Fleischer, Cornell H. *Bureaucrat and Intellectual in the Ottoman Empire: The Historian Mustafa Ali (1541–1600)*. Princeton: Princeton University Press, 1986.

——. "The Lawgiver as Messiah: The Making of the Imperial Image in the Reign of Süleyman." In *Soliman le Magnifique et son temps*, edited by Gilles Veinstein, pp. 159–77. Paris: La Documentation Française, 1992.

Goffman, Daniel. *The Ottoman Empire and Early Modern Europe*. Cambridge and New York: Cambridge University Press, 2002.

Goodrich, Thomas D. "Atlas-ı Hümayun: A Sixteenth-Century Ottoman Maritime Atlas Discovered in 1984." *Archivum Ottomanicum* 10 (1985): 83–101.

——. "The Earliest Ottoman Maritime Atlas – The Walters Deniz atlası." *Archivum Ottomanicum* 11 (1986): 25–50.

——. "Old Maps in the Library of Topkapi Palace in Istanbul." *Imago Mundi* 45 (1993): 120–33.

——. "Ottoman Americana: The Search for the Sources of the Sixteenth-century *Tarih-i Hindi-i Garbi*." *Bulletin of Research in the Humanities* 85 (1982): 269–94.

——. *The Ottoman Turks and the New World: A Study of Tarih-i Hindi-i Garbi and Sixteenth-Century Ottoman Americana.* Wiesbaden: Harrassowitz, 1990.

——. "Some Unpublished Sixteenth Century Ottoman Maps." In *Actes du VIᵉ congrès du C.I.E.P.O. tenu à Cambridge sur les provinces arabes à l'époque ottomane*, edited by the Comité international d'études pré-ottomanes et ottomanes and Abdeljelil Temimi, pp. 99–103. Zaghouan, Tunisia: Centre d'études et de recherches ottomanes et morisco-andalouses, 1984.

——. "*Tarih-i Hindi-i Garbi*: An Ottoman Book on the New World." *Journal of the American Oriental Society* 107 (1987): 317–19.

Green, John. *The Construction of Maps and Globes ....* London: Printed for T. Horne, J. Knapton, R. Knaplock, J. Wyat, et al., 1717.

Greene, Molly. "Resurgent Islam: 1500–1700." In *The Mediterranean in History*, edited by David Anulafia, pp. 219–51. London: Thames & Hudson, 2003.

Grundy, Isobel. *Lady Mary Wortley Montagu*. Oxford: Oxford University Press, 1999.

Hagen, Gottfried. "Katip Çelebi and Tarih-i Hind-i Garbi." *Güney-Doğu Avrupa Araştırmaları Dergisi* 12 (1998): 101–15.

——. "Some Considerations on the Study of Ottoman Geographical Writings." *Archivum Ottomanicum* 18 (2000): 183–94.

Harley, J. Brian. "Silences and Secrecy: The Hidden Agenda of Cartography in Early Modern Europe." *Imago Mundi* 40 (1988): 57–76.

Hess, Andrew C. "The Evolution of the Ottoman Seaborne Empire in the Age of Oceanic Discoveries, 1453–1525." *American Historical Review* 75 (1970): 1892–1919.

——. "Piri Reis and the Ottoman Response to the Voyages of Discovery." *Terrae Incognitae* 6 (1974): 19–37.

Howard, Deborah. "The Status of the Oriental Traveller in Renaissance Venice." In *Re-Orienting the Renaissance: Cultural Exchanges with the East*, edited by Gerald Maclean, pp. 29–49. Basingstoke, England: Palgrave Macmillan, 2005.

İnalcık, Halil. "The Ottoman State: Economy and Society, 1300–1600." In *An Economic and Social History of the Ottoman Empire*, edited by Halil İnalcık with Donald Quataert, pp. 271–315. Cambridge: Cambridge University Press, 1994

——. "The Policy of Mehmed II towards the Greek Population of Istanbul and the Byzantine Buildings of the City." *Dumbarton Oaks Papers* 23 (1970): 231–49.

Jardine, Lisa. *Worldly Goods*. London: Macmillan, 1996.

Kafesçioğlu, Çiğdem. "The Ottoman Capital in the Making: The Reconstruction of Constantinople in the 15th Century." Ph.D. dissertation, Harvard University, 1996.

Kahane, Henry; Renée Kahana; and Andreas Tietze. *The Lingua Franca in the Levant: Turkish Nautical Terms of Italian and Greek Origin*. Urbana: University of Illinois Press, 1958.

Kahle, Paul E. "Eine Islamische Quelle über China um 1500 (Das Khitayname des Ali Ekber)." In Reprint of *Text and Studies on the Historical Geography and Topography of East Asia*, edited by Fuat Sezgin et al., pp. 379–98. Islamic Geography 126. Frankfurt am Main: Institute for the History of Arabic-Islamic Science at the Johann Wolfgang Goethe University, 1993.

Karamustafa, Ahmet T. "Military, Administrative, and Scholarly Maps and Plans." In *The History of Cartography*, Vol. 2, Book 1: *Cartography in the Traditional Islamic and South Asian Societies*, edited by J. B. Harley and David Woodward, pp. 209–28. Chicago: University of Chicago Press, 1992.

Karrow, Robert W., Jr. *Mapmakers of the Sixteenth Century and Their Maps: Bio-Bibliographies of the Cartographers of Abraham Ortelius, 1570.* Chicago: Published for The Newberry by Speculum Orbis Press, 1993.

King, David A. *Islamic Astronomical Instruments.* London: Variorum Reprints, 1987.

Kish, George. "The Cosmographic Heart: Cordiform Maps of the 16th Century." *Imago Mundi* 19 (1965): 13–21.

Koeman, Cornelis. *Atlantes Neerlandici: Bibliography of Terrestrial, Maritime, and Celestial Atlases and Pilot Books, Published in The Netherlands up to 1800.* 5 volumes. Amsterdam: Theatrum Orbis Terrarum, 1967–1971.

Konvitz, Josef W. *Cartography in France, 1660–1848: Science, Engineering, and Statecraft.* Chicago: University of Chicago Press, 1987.

Kreiser, Klaus. "Evliya Çelebi." October 2005. http://www.ottomanhistorians.com/database/html/evliya_en.html

Krokar, James P. *The Ottoman Presence in Southeastern Europe, 16th–19th Centuries: A View in Maps.* The Newberry Library Slide Set Number 27. Chicago: The Newberry Library, 1997.

Kuntz, Marion L. *Guillaume Postel: Prophet of the Restitution of All Things – His Life and Thought.* The Hague: Martinus Nijhoff Publishers, 1981.

Lach, Donald F. *Asia in the Making of Europe.* Chicago: University of Chicago Press, 1965.

Lewis, Bernard. "Ottoman Observers of Ottoman Decline." *Islamic Studies* 1 (1962): 71–87.

Liu, Yih-Min. "A Comparative and Critical Study of Ali Akbar's Khitay-nama with Reference to Chinese Sources." *Central Asiatic Journal* 27 (1983): 58–78.

Livingstone, David N. *The Geographical Tradition: Episodes in the History of a Contested Enterprise.* Oxford: Blackwell, 1992.

Lockman, Zachary. *Contending Visions of the Middle East: The History and Politics of Orientalism.* Cambridge and New York: Cambridge University Press, 2004.

MacLean, Gerald, editor. *Re-Orienting the Renaissance: Cultural Exchanges with the East.* Basingstoke, England and New York: Palgrave Macmillan, 2005.

——. *The Rise of Oriental Travel: English Visitors to the Ottoman Empire, 1580–1720.* Basingstoke, England and New York: Palgrave Macmillan, 2004.

Mangani, Giorgio. "Abraham Ortelius and the Hermetic Meaning of the Cordiform Projection." *Imago Mundi* 50 (1998): 59–82.

Manners, Ian R. "Constructing the Image of a City: The Representation of Constantinople in Christopher Buondelmonti's '*Liber Insularum Archipelagi.*'" *Annals of the Association of American Geographers* 87 (1997): 72–102.

Mansell, Philip. "The French Renaissance in Search of the Ottoman Empire." In *Re-Orienting the Renaissance: Cultural Exchanges with the East*, edited by Gerald Maclean, pp. 96–107. Basingstoke, England: Palgrave Macmillan, 2005.

Ménage, V. L. "The Map of Hajji Ahmed and Its Makers." *Bulletin of the School of Oriental and African Studies, University of London* 21 (1958): 291–314.

Miquel, A. "Al- Iṣṭakhrī, abū Isḥāḳ Ibrāhīm b. Muḥammad al-Fārisī al-Karkhī." *Encyclopaedia of Islam*, edited by P. Bearman, Th. Bianquis, C. E. Bosworth, E. van Donzel, and W. P. Heinrichs. Brill, 2007. Brill Online. University of Chicago Libraries. 10 August 2007. http://www.brillonline.nl.proxy.uchicago.edu/subscriber/entry?entry=islam_SIM-3673.

Miller, Naomi. *Mapping the City: The Language and Culture of Cartography in The Renaissance.* London and New York: Continuum, 2003.

Mollat du Jourdin, Michel, and Monique de La Roncière. *Sea Charts of the Early Explorers: 13th to 17th Century*. New York: Thames & Hudson, 1984.

Mordtmann, J. H. "Das Observatorium des Taqi ed-din zu Pera." In *Arabische Instrumente in orientalischen Studien*, Vol. 4: *Astronomische Instrumente Publikationen, 1918–1925*, edited by Fuat Sezgin, pp. 281–95. Veröffentlichungen des Instituts für Geschichte der Arabisch-Islamischen Wissenschaften, Reihe B. Frankfurt am Main: Johann Wolfgang Goethe-University, 1991.

Murphey, Rhoads. "Bigots or Informed Observers? A Periodization of Pre-Colonial English and European Writing on the Middle East." *Journal of the American Oriental Society* 110 (1990): 291–303.

Necipoğlu, Gülru. *Architecture, Ceremonial, and Power: The Topkapı Palace in the Fifteenth and Sixteenth Centuries*. Cambridge: M.I.T. Press, 1991.

Nuti, L. "The Perspective Plan in the Sixteenth Century: The Invention of a Representational Language." *The Art Bulletin* 76 (1994): 105–28.

O'Sullivan, Dan. *The Age of Discovery, 1400–1550*. London and New York: Longman, 1984.

Özdemir, Kemal. *Ottoman Nautical Charts: The Atlas of Ali Macar Reis*. Translated by P. Mary Işın. Istanbul: Marmara Bank Publication, 1992.

Özen, Mine Esiner. *Piri Reis and His Charts*. Istanbul: N. Refioğlu, 1998.

Parks, George B. "The Contents and Sources of Ramusio's *Navigationi*." *Bulletin of the New York Public Library* 59 (1955): 279–313.

Parr, Charles McKew. *Jan van Linschoten: The Dutch Marco Polo*. New York: Thomas Y. Crowell, 1964.

Pastoureau, Mireille. "French School Atlases: Sixteenth to Eighteenth Centuries." In *Images of the World: The Atlas Through History*, edited by John A. Wolter and Ronald E. Grim, pp. 109–34. New York: McGraw-Hill, 1997.

——. *Nicolas Sanson d'Abbeville: Atlas du Monde, 1665*. Paris: Sand & Conti, 1988.

——. *Les Sansons (1630–1730): Un siècle de cartographie Française*. Paris: Sand & Conti, 1981.

Penrose, Boies. *Travel and Discovery in the Renaissance, 1420–1620*. Cambridge, MA: Harvard University Press, 1952.

Phillips, Carl. "Introduction." In *A Voyage to Arabia Felix (1708–1710); and, A Journey from Mocha to Muab (1711–13); and, A Narrative Concerning Coffee; and, An Historical Treatise Concerning Coffee*, by Jean de La Roque, pp. vii–xxiv. Cambridge: Oleander, 2004.

Pinto, John A. "Origins and Development of the Ichnographic City Plan." *Journal of the Society of Architectural Historians* 35 (1976): 35–50.

Pinto, Karen C. "Ways of Seeing: Scenarios of the World in the Medieval Islamic Cartographic Imagination." Ph.D. dissertation, Columbia University, 2001.

Quataert, Donald. *The Ottoman Empire, 1700–1922*. Cambridge: Cambridge University Press, 2000.

Rees, Ronald. "Historical Links between Cartography and Art." *Geographical Review* 70 (1980): 60–78.

Reinhartz, Dennis. *The Cartographer and the Literati – Herman Moll and His Intellectual Circle*. Lampeter: Edwin Mellen Press, 1997.

Renda, Günsel. "Representations of Towns in Ottoman Sea Charts of the Sixteenth Century and Their Relation to Mediterranean Cartography." In *Soliman le Magnifique et son temps: Actes du Colloque de Paris, Galeries Nationales du Grand Palais, 7–10 mars 1990*, edited by Gilles Veinstein, pp. 279–97. Paris: Documentation Française, 1992.

Rogers, J. M. "Itineraries and Town Views in Ottoman Histories." In *The History of Cartography*. Vol. 2, Book 1: *Cartography in the Traditional Islamic and South Asian Societies*, edited by J. B. Harley and David Woodward, pp. 228–55. Chicago: University of Chicago Press, 1992.

de la Roque, Jean. *A Voyage to Arabia the Happy, By Way of the Eastern Ocean and the Red Sea*. London: Printed for G. Strahan ... and R. Williamson, 1726.

Roth, Cecil. "Judah Abenzara's Map of the Mediterranean World, 1500." *Studies in Bibliography and Booklore* 9 (1970): 116-20.

Saliba, George. "The Role of the Astrologer in Medieval Islamic Society." *Bulletin d'Études Orientales* 44 (1992): 45-67.

Sayılı, Adnan. *The Observatory in Islam and Its Place in the General History of Observatory.* Ankara: TTK, 1960.

Schefer, Charles. "Trois chapitres du Khitay Nameh: Texte persan et traduction française." In Reprint of *Text and Studies on the Historical Geography and Topography of East Asia,* edited by Fuat Sezgin et al., pp. 159-214. Islamic Geography 126. Frankfurt am Main: Institute for the History of Arabic-Islamic Science at the Johann Wolfgang Goethe University, 1993.

Schulz, Juergen. "Jacopo de'Barbari's View of Venice: Mapmaking, City Views, and Moralized Geography before the Year 1500." *The Art Bulletin* 60 (1978): 425-74.

——. "Maps as Metaphors: Mural Map Cycles of the Italian Renaissance." In *Art and Cartography: Six Historical Essays,* edited by David Woodward, pp. 97-122. Chicago: University of Chicago Press, 1987.

Skelton, R. A. "Background Notes" to G. *de Jode Speculum Orbis Terrarum.* Amsterdam: Theatrum Orbis Terrarum, 1965.

——. "Introduction" to *Civitates Orbis Terrarum: 'The Towns of the World,' 1572-1617.* Amsterdam: Theatrum Orbis Terrarum, 1966.

Soucek, Svat. "The 'Ali Macar Reis Atlas' and the Deniz Kitabı: Their Place in the Genre of Portolan Charts and Atlases." *Imago Mundi* 25 (1971): 17-27.

——. "Islamic Charting in the Mediterranean." In *The History of Cartography,* Vol. 2, Book 1: *Cartography in the Traditional Islamic and South Asian Societies,* edited by J. B. Harley and David Woodward, pp. 263-92. Chicago: University of Chicago Press, 1992.

——. "Pīrī Reʾīs b. Ḥādjdjī Meḥmed." *Encyclopaedia of Islam,* edited by P. Bearman, Th. Bianquis, C. E. Bosworth, E. van Donzel, and W. P. Heinrichs. Brill, 2007. Brill Online. University of Chicago Libraries. 10 August 2007. http://www.brillonline.nl.proxy.uchicago.edu/subscriber/entry?entry=islam_SIM-6126.

Stoye, John. *Marsigli's Europe, 1680-1730: The Life and Times of Luigi Ferdinando Marsigli, Soldier and Virtuoso.* New Haven: Yale University Press, 1994.

Sundeen, Glenn. "Thévenot the Tourist: A Frenchman Abroad in the Ottoman Empire." In *Distant Lands and Diverse Cultures: The French Experience in Asia, 1600-1700,* edited by Glenn J. Ames and Ronald S. Love, pp. 1-20. Westport: Praeger, 2003.

Thrower, Norman J. W. *Maps and Civilization: Cartography in Culture and Society.* London: University of Chicago Press, 1996.

Tibbetts, Gerald R. *Arabia in Early Maps: A Bibliography of Maps Covering the Peninsula of Arabia, Printed in Western Europe from the Invention of Printing to the Year 1751.* New York: Oleander, 1978.

——. "The Balkhi School of Geographers." In *The History of Cartography,* Vol. 2, Book 1: *Cartography in the Traditional Islamic and South Asian Societies,* edited by J. B. Harley and David Woodward, pp. 108-36. Chicago: University of Chicago Press, 1992.

Türkay, Cevdet. *Osmanlı Türklerinde Coğrafya.* Istanbul: Maarif, 1959.

Turnbull, David. "Cartography and Science in Early Modern Europe: Mapping the Construction of Knowledge Spaces." *Imago Mundi* 48 (1996): 5-24.

Turner, Hilary Louise. "Christopher Buondelmonti and the Isolario." *Terrae Incognita* 19 (1987): 11-28.

Vatin, Nicolas. *Rodos Şövalyeleri ve Osmanlılar: Doğu Akdeniz'de Savaş Diplomasi ve Korsanlık: 1480-1522.* Translated by Tülin Altınova. Istanbul: Türkiye Ekonomik ve Toplumsal Tarih Vakfı, 2004.

Vedovato, Mirco. "The Nautical Chart of Mohammed Raus, 1590." *Imago Mundi* 8 (1951): 49.

Watson, William J. "Ibrahim Müterferrika and Turkish Incunabula" *Journal of the American Oriental Society* 88 (1968): 435–41.

Whitfield, Peter. *The Charting of the Oceans: Ten Centuries of Maritime Maps*. London: The British Library, 1996.

Wolff, Larry. *Inventing Eastern Europe: The Map of Civilization on the Mind of the Enlightenment*. Stanford: Stanford University Press, 1994.

Yerasimos, Stephane. "Osmanlı İstanbul'unun Kuruluşu." In *Osmanlı Mimarlığının 7 Yüzyılı "Olağanüstü Bir Miras,"* edited by Nur Akın et al., pp. 195–212. Istanbul: Librairie d'Amérique et d'Orient, 1999.

——. *Les voyageurs dans l'empire Ottoman (XIVᵉ–XVIᵉ siècles)*. Ankara: Imprimerie de la Société Turque d'Histoire, 1991.

York, Anne. "Travels in India: Jean-Baptiste Tavernier." In *Distant Lands and Diverse Cultures: The French Experience in Asia, 1600–1700*, edited by Glenn J. Ames and Ronald S. Love, pp. 135–46. Westport: Praeger, 2003.

Zenker, J. Th. "Das chinesische Reich, nach dem türkischen Khatainame." In Reprint of *Text and Studies on the Historical Geography and Topography of East Asia*, edited by Fuat Sezgin et al., pp. 109–29. Islamic Geography 126. Frankfurt am Main: Institute for the History of Arabic-Islamic Science at the Johann Wolfgang Goethe University, 1993.

CHECKLIST TO THE EXHIBIT

INTRODUCTION

[*A Complete and Perfect Map Describing the Whole World*] (translated from the Turkish title). [1559] 1795
[Hajji Ahmed]
The Newberry Library, Chicago, Franco Novacco Map Collection

GROUP 1: RENAISSANCE CARTOGRAPHY AND THE "REDISCOVERY" OF PTOLEMY'S *GEOGRAPHIA*

Geographia. 1482
Francesco di Nicolò Berlinghieri
Florence
The Newberry Library, Chicago, Gift of Edward E. Ayer

Prima Asie Tabvla. 1486
[Claudius Ptolemy]
Ulm
The O. J. Sopranos Collection

Prima Asiae Tabvla and (verso) sections of *Secvnda Asiae Tabvla.* 1511
Bernardus Sylvanus
Venice
The O. J. Sopranos Collection

Tabula noua Asiae minoris. 1541
Lorenz Fries
Viennae
The O. J. Sopranos Collection

GROUP 2: THE WORLD OBSERVED AND ENCOMPASSED

Il disegno della prima parte del Asia 1559
Il disegno seconda parte dell'Asia 1561
Giacomo Gastaldi
Venice
The Newberry Library, Chicago, Franco Novacco Map Collection

Tvrcia Tvrcicive Imperii seu Solij mannorum regni pleraque pars, nunc recens summa fide ac industria elucubrata. From *Specvlvm Orbis Terrarvm. Antverpiae.* 1578
Gerard de Jode
Amsterdam
The O. J. Sopranos Collection

Tvrcici Imperii Descriptio. [1579] 1602. From *Theatrum Orbis Terrarum*
Abraham Ortelius
Amsterdam
The O. J. Sopranos Collection

Tvrcicvm Imperivm. [1635] 1680?
Frederick de Witt
Amsterdam
The O. J. Sopranos Collection

Delle Navigationi et Viaggi, Roccolto da M. Gio. Batt. Ramvsio & con molti vaghi discorsi .... Primo volume, & Seconda
editione. Venetia: Stamperia de Givnti, 1554
Giovanni Battista Ramusio
Venice
The University of Chicago Library, Special Collections Research Center

Tarih-i Hind-i Garbi [*History of the India of the West*]. Ca. 1600
Anonymous
The Newberry Library, Chicago, Gift of Edward E. Ayer

GROUP 3: ENLIGHTENED FRENCH CARTOGRAPHY

Carte de L'Empire des Tvrcs et ses confins. 1664
Pierre du Val
Paris
The O. J. Sopranos Collection

*The Turkish Empire in Europe, Asia and Africa, Dividid into all its Governments, together with the other Territories that are
Tributary to it, as also the Dominions of ye Emperor of Marocco. According to the Newest and most Exact Observations.* 1720
Herman Moll
London
The O. J. Sopranos Collection

*Carte particuliere de la Hongrie, de la Transilvanie, de la Croatie, et de la Sclavonie, Dressée sur les Observations de M^r. le
Comte Marsilli et sur plusieurs autre Memoires.* 1717
Guillaume de L'Isle
Paris
The Newberry Library, Chicago, John Gabriel Sack Map Collection

*Carte de la Turquie de l'Arabie et de la Perse. Dressée sur les Memoires les plus recens rectifiez par les Observations de Mrs. de
l'Academie Royle des Sciences.* 1745
Guillaume de L'Isle
Amsterdam
The O. J. Sopranos Collection

[*General Atlas: A Collection of Large-Scale Maps and Charts of All Parts of the World by Various Cartographers and
Publishers*]. [1816?]
William Faden
London
The Newberry Library, Chicago, Gift of Edward E. Ayer

Les Estats de l'Empire des Turqs en Asie. 1652
Nicolas Sanson
Paris
The O. J. Sopranos Collection

[*Map of the Western Mediterranean*]. 1803. From *Cedid atlas tercümesi* [*Translation of the New Atlas*]. 1803
Üsküdar [Istanbul]
The Newberry Library, Chicago, Gift of Roger S. Baskes

GROUP 4: THE MEDITERRANEAN TRADITION OF CHARTING

Manuscript Portolan Chart of the Mediterranean and Black Seas. 1568
Domenico Oliva
—
The Newberry Library, Chicago, Gift of Edward E. Ayer

Walters Deniz atlası [*Walters Sea Atlas*]. Ca. 1560
Anonymous
—
The Walters Art Museum, Baltimore

Manuscript Portolan Atlas of the Mediterranean and African Coast. 1583
Joan Martines
—
The Newberry Library, Chicago, Gift of Edward E. Ayer

Thalassografica Tabula totius Maris Mediterranei. 1595
Willem Barentsz
Amsterdam
The O. J. Sopranos Collection

Vera dichiaratione del Mare del Archipelago con tutti soi insuli, porti, spiaggie, e secci &c. Portatato in luce da Pietro Silvestro Valck. 1676
Hendrick Doncker
Amsterdam
The O. J. Sopranos Collection

Prima Parte dello Specchio del Mare. 1664
Francisco Maria Levanto
Genoa
The O. J. Sopranos Collection

Carte Nouvelle de la Mer Mediterranee où sont Exactement Remarqués tous les Ports, Golfes, Rochers, Bancs de Sable &c. a l'usage des Armées du Roy de la Grande Bretagne. [1694] 1711
Romeijn de Hooghe
Amsterdam
The O. J. Sopranos Collection

GROUP 5: MAPPING THE CITY

[*Constantinople*]. 1493. From the *Liber Chronicarum*. 1493
Hartmann Schedel
Nuremberg
The O. J. Sopranos Collection

Tvnes, Oppidvm Barbarie .... 1575. From *Civitates Orbis Terrarum*. 1572–1617/1633?
Georg Braun and Frans Hogenberg
Cologne?
The University of Chicago Library, Special Collections Research Center

Byzantivm nunc Constantinopolis. 1572. From *Civitates Orbis Terrarum*. 1572
Georg Braun and Frans Hogenberg
Cologne
The O. J. Sopranos Collection

Cairos, quae olim Babylon Aegypti maxima vrbs. 1575. From *Civitates Orbis Terrarum*. 1575
Georg Braun and Frans Hogenberg
Cologne
The O. J. Sopranos Collection

Alexandria vetustissimum Ægÿpti emporium.... 1575. From *Civitates Orbis Terrarum*. 1575
Georg Braun and Frans Hogenberg
Cologne
The O. J. Sopranos Collection.

Damascvs, vrbs noblissima ad Libanum montem, Totius Sÿriæ Metropolis. 1575. From *Civitates Orbis Terrarum*. 1575
Georg Braun and Frans Hogenberg
Cologne
The O. J. Sopranos Collection

Constantinopolis .... 1641. From *De Rebuspublicus Hanseaticis*. 1641
Matthäus Merian
Frankfurt
The O. J. Sopranos Collection

Kitab dala'il al-khairat wa shawariq al-anwar fi dkikh al-salat 'ala al-nabiyy al-mukhtar. 1764–1765
Ahmad Ardarumi [Ahmad of Erzurum?].
—
The Oriental Institute Museum, OIM A12048

Plan de la Ville de Constantinople et de ses Faubourgs tant en Europe qu'en Asie levé géometriquement en 1776. [1776] 1822
Fr. Kauffer
Paris
The O. J. Sopranos Collection

GROUP 6: THROUGH THE EYES OF TRAVELERS

Christoph. Buondelmonti, Florentini, Librum insularum archipelagi .... [Ca. 1418] 1824
[Christopher Buondelmonti] G. R. L. Von Sinner
Leipzig and Berlin
The University of Chicago Library, Special Collections Research Center

Rhodis. 1486. From *Peregrinatio in Terram Sanctam*. 1486
[Erhard Reuwich]
Mainz
The O. J. Sopranos Collection

Peregrinatio in Terram Sanctam. 1490
Bernhard von Breydenbach
Speier
The University of Chicago Library, Special Collections Research Center

Le Navigationi et Viaggi, fatti nella Turchia 1580
Nicolas de Nicolay
Venice
The O. J. Sopranos Collection

Deliniatuur in hac tabula, Orae maritimae Abexiae, freti Meccani, al Maris Rubri, Arabiae .... 1596. From *Itinerario, Voyage ofte Schipvaert van Jan Huygen van Linschoten naar Oost-ofte Portugalis Indien. 1563–1611*
Jan Huygen van Linschoten
Amsterdam
The O. J. Sopranos Collection

Les six Voyages de Jean Baptiste Tavernier 1677
Jean-Baptiste Tavernier
Paris
The University of Chicago Library, Special Collections Research Center

Reizen van Cornelis de Bruyn, door de Vermaardtse Deelen van Klein Asie 1698
Cornelis De Bruijn
Delft
The O. J. Sopranos Collection

Voyage de l'Arabie heureuse ..., fait par les françois pour la premiere fois, dans les années 1708, 1709 & 1710 ...; avec ... un memoire concernant l'arbre & le fruit du café 1716
Jean de la Roque
Paris
The University of Chicago Library, Special Collections Research Center

Voyage fait par ordre du Roy Louis XIV dans la Palestine: vers le Grand Emir, chef des princes arabes du desert ... Par D. L. R. [de la Roque]. [1717] 1732
Laurent d'Arvieux, Chevalier
Paris
The University of Chicago Library, Special Collections Research Center

Letters of the Right Honourable Lady M–y W–y M–e, Written During Her Travels in Europe, Asia, and Africa, to Persons of Distinction, Men of Letters, &c. in Different Parts of Europe 1764
Lady Mary Wortley Montagu
London
The University of Chicago Library, Special Collections Research Center

Description de l'Arabie, d'aprés les observations et recherches faites dans le pays meme 1773
Carsten Niebuhr
Paris
The University of Chicago Library, Special Collections Research Center

Voyage pittoresque de la Grece, Volume 1. 1782
M. G. F. A. Comte de Choiseul-Gouffier
Paris
The O. J. Sopranos Collection

Voyage en Syrie et en Égypte: pendant les années 1783, 1784 et 1785. 1792
M. Constantin-François Volney
Paris
The University of Chicago Library, Special Collections Research Center

INDEX OF CARTOGRAPHERS AND GEOGRAPHERS